Level 2 • Book 1

Themes

Kindness

Let's Explore

Around the Town

SRA Imagine It!

Level 2
Book 1

Program Authors

Carl Bereiter
Andy Biemiller
Joe Campione
Iva Carruthers
Doug Fuchs
Lynn Fuchs
Steve Graham
Karen Harris

Jan Hirshberg
Anne McKeough
Peter Pannell
Michael Pressley
Marsha Roit
Marlene Scardamalia
Marcy Stein
Gerald H. Treadway Jr.

McGraw Hill SRA

Columbus, OH

Acknowledgments

Grateful acknowledgement is given to the following publishers and copyright owners for permissions granted to reprint selections from their publications. All possible care has been taken to trace ownership and secure permission for each selection included. In case of any errors or omissions, the Publisher will be pleased to make suitable acknowledgements in future editions.

KINDNESS

BECAUSE OF YOU. Text copyright © 2005 by B.G. Hennessy. Illustrations copyright © 2005 by Hiroe Nakata. Reproduced by permission of the publisher Candlewick Press, Inc., Cambridge, MA.
FOR THE LOVE OF OUR EARTH by P. K. Hallinan. Copyright © 1992 by the author. Reprinted by permission of Ideals Publications, LLC.
"The Lion and the Mouse" Reprinted with the permission of Margaret K. McElderry Books, an imprint of Simon & Schuster Children's Publishing Division from THE MCELDERRY BOOK OF AESOP'S FABLES by Michael Morpurgo. Text copyright © 2004 Michael Morpurgo.
From CORDUROY by Don Freeman, copyright © 1968 by Don Freeman. Used by permission of Viking Penguin, an imprint of Penguin Putnam Books for Young Readers, a division of Penguin Putnam Inc. All rights reserved including the right of reproduction in whole or in part in any form. This edition published by arrangement with Viking Children's Books, a member of Penguin Young Readers Group, a division of Penguin Group (USA) Inc.
"dear tulips," from DEAR WORLD by Takayo Noda, copyright © 2003 by Takayo Noda. Used by permission of Dial Books for Young Readers, A Division of Penguin Young Readers Group, A Member of Penguin Group (USA) Inc., 345 Hudson Street, New York, NY 10014. All rights reserved.
"Sick Days" From FATHERS, MOTHERS, SISTERS, BROTHERS by MARY ANN HOBERMAN. Copyright © 1991 by Mary Ann Hoberman (Text); Copyright © 1991 by Marilyn Hafner (Illustrations). By permission of Little, Brown and Co., Inc.

LET'S EXPLORE

ANTS! THEY ARE HARD WORKERS! By Editors of Time for Kids with Brenda Iasevoli. COPYRIGHT © 2005. Used by permission of HarperCollins.
IF YOU FIND A ROCK, text copyright © 2000 by Peggy Christian, photographs copyright © 2000 by Barbara Hirsch Lember, reprinted by permission of Harcourt, Inc. This material may not be reproduced in any form or by any means without the prior written permission of the publisher.
HUNGRY HOPPERS: GRASSHOPPERS IN YOUR BACKYARD by Nancy Loewen, illustrated by Brandon Reibeling. Used with permission from Picture Window Books.
BIRDHOUSE FOR RENT by Harriet Ziefert, illustrated by Donald Dreifuss. Text copyright © 2001 by Harriet Ziefert. Illustrations copyright © 2001 by Donald Dreifuss. Reprinted by permission of Houghton Mifflin Company. All rights reserved.
From TELL ME, TREE by GAIL GIBBONS. Copyright © 2002 by Gail Gibbons. By permission of Little, Brown & Co., Inc.
"Ants" Reprinted with the permission of Atheneum Books for Young Readers, an imprint of Simon & Schuster Children's Publishing Division from FIREFLIES AT MIDNIGHT by Marilyn Singer. Text copyright © 2003 Marilyn Singer.

AROUND THE TOWN

From RED LIGHT, GREEN LIGHT, MAMA AND ME by Cari Best, Illustrated by Niki Daly. Published by Scholastic Inc./Orchard Books. Text copyright © 1995 by Cari Best, illustrations copyright © 1995 by Niki Daly. All rights reserved. Used by permission of Scholastic Inc.
IN THE MONEY © 2006 by Picture Window Books. All rights reserved.
From JALAPENO BAGELS by Natasha Wing, illustrated by Robert Casilla. Text Copyright © 1996 by Natasha Wing, Illustrations Copyright © 1996 by Robert Casilla. Reprinted by arrangement with Atheneum Books for Young Readers, an Imprint of Simon & Schuster Children's Publishing Division. All rights reserved.
OUT AND ABOUT AT CITY HALL © 2006 by Picture Window Books. All rights reserved.
GRANDPA'S CORNER STORE by DyAnne DiSalvo-Ryan. COPYRIGHT © 2000 BY DYANNE DISALVO-RYAN. Used by permission of HarperCollins Publishers.
"Supermarket" by Lois Lenski from CITY POEMS. Used by permission.
From ONCE INSIDE THE LIBRARY by Barbara Huff. Copyright © 1957 by Barbara A Huff (Text): Copyright © renewed 1985 by Barbara A. Huff (Text): Copyright © 1990 by Iris Van Ryanbach (Illustrations). By permission of Little, Brown and Co., Inc. All rights reserved. To purchase copies of this book, please call 1.800.759.0190.

SRAonline.com

Program Authors

Carl Bereiter, Ph.D.
University of Toronto

Andy Biemiller, Ph.D.
University of Toronto

Joe Campione, Ph.D.
University of California, Berkeley

Iva Carruthers, Ph.D.
Northeastern Illinois University

Doug Fuchs, Ph.D.
Vanderbilt University

Lynn Fuchs, Ph.D.
Vanderbilt University

Steve Graham, Ed.D.
Vanderbilt University

Karen Harris, Ed.D.
Vanderbilt University

Jan Hirshberg, Ed.D.
Reading Specialist

Anne McKeough, Ph.D.
University of Toronto

Peter Pannell
Principal, Longfellow Elementary School,
Pasadena, California

Michael Pressley, Ph.D.
Michigan State University

Marsha Roit, Ed.D.
National Reading Consultant

Marlene Scardamalia, Ph.D.
University of Toronto

Marcy Stein, Ph.D.
University of Washington, Tacoma

Gerald H. Treadway, Jr., Ed.D.
San Diego State University

Unit 1 Table of Contents

Kindness

Unit Overview ⋯⋯⋯⋯⋯➤ 12

Vocabulary Warm-Up ⋯⋯⋯⋯➤ 14

Because of You ⋯⋯⋯⋯➤ 16
fiction written by B. G. Hennessy • *illustrated by* Hiroe Nakata

Meet the Author, B. G. Hennessy
Meet the Illustrator, Hiroe Nakata ⋯⋯⋯➤ 30

Theme Connections ⋯⋯⋯⋯➤ 31

🌐 **Social Studies** Inquiry The Life of Clara Barton ⋯⋯➤ 32

Vocabulary Warm-Up ⋯⋯⋯⋯⋯➤ 34

For the Love of Our Earth ⋯⋯➤ 36
rhyming fiction written and illustrated by P. K. Hallinan

Meet the Author/Illustrator, P. K. Hallinan ⋯⋯⋯➤ 52

Theme Connections ⋯⋯⋯⋯⋯➤ 53

🌐 **Social Studies** Inquiry Schools to Celebrate Earth Day ⋯⋯➤ 54

Vocabulary Warm-Up ⋯⋯⋯⋯➤ 56

The Elves and the Shoemaker ⋯⋯⋯➤ 58
fairy tale by Brothers Grimm, *retold by* Emily Greggs and Bethany Martin • *illustrated by* Viktor Shatunov

Meet the Authors, Brothers Grimm
Meet the Illustrator, Viktor Shatunov ⋯⋯➤ 76

Theme Connections ⋯⋯⋯⋯➤ 77

🌐 **Social Studies** Inquiry Trade ⋯⋯➤ 78

Vocabulary Warm-Up ....➤ 80

The Lion and the Mouse ....➤ 82

fable retold by Michael Morpurgo •
illustrated by Emma Chichester Clark

Meet the Author, Michael Morpurgo
Award-winning author

Meet the Illustrator, Emma Chichester Clark ......➤ 92
Award-winning illustrator

Theme Connections ....➤ 93

Science Inquiry Survival ....➤ 94

Vocabulary Warm-Up ....➤ 96

Corduroy ....➤ 98

fantasy written and illustrated by Don Freeman

Meet the Author/Illustrator, Don Freeman ....➤ 116
Award-winning author

Theme Connections ....➤ 117

Social Studies Inquiry Lunch Money .....➤ 118

dear tulips ....➤ 120

poem written and illustrated by Takayo Noda

Sick Days ....➤ 122

poem by Mary Ann Hoberman •
illustrated by Marylin Hafner

Test Prep ....➤ 124

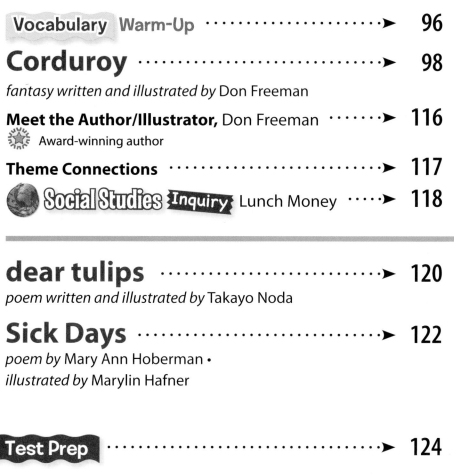

Unit 2 Table of Contents

Let's Expore

Unit Overview ·······························➤ **128**

Vocabulary Warm-Up ······················➤ **130**

Ants! They are hard workers! ···········➤ **132**
expository text by the Editors of TIME for Kids, with Brenda Iasevoli

Meet the Author, Brenda Iasevoli ··········➤ **154**

Theme Connections ······················➤ **155**

Science Inquiry From Eggs to Butterflies ··➤ **156**

Vocabulary Warm-Up ·······················➤ **158**

If You Find a Rock ⭐ John Burroughs
Award for Nature Writing for Children, 2000 ··············➤ **160**
nonfiction by Peggy Christian • *photographs by* Barbara Hirsch Lember

Meet the Author, Peggy Christian
Meet the Photographer, Barbara Hirsch Lember ··➤ **182**

Theme Connections ························➤ **183**

Science Inquiry A Story from the Past ····➤ **184**

Vocabulary Warm-Up ···············➤ **186**

Hungry Hoppers ················➤ **188**
expository text by Nancy Loewen • *illustrated by* Brandon Reibeling

Meet the Author, Nancy Loewen
Meet the Illustrator, Brandon Reibeling ······➤ **208**

Theme Connections ·················➤ **209**

Science Inquiry From Tadpole to Frog ➤ **210**

Vocabulary Warm-Up ···················➤ 212

Birdhouse for Rent ···············➤ 214

fiction by Harriet Ziefert • *illustrated by* Donald Dreifuss

Meet the Author, Harriet Ziefert ⭐ Award-winning author
Meet the Illustrator, Donald Dreifuss ···········➤ 240

Theme Connections ·······················➤ 241

Science Inquiry The Weather Lesson ·····➤ 242

Vocabulary Warm-Up ·················➤ 244

Tell Me, Tree ·················➤ 246

expository text written and illustrated by Gail Gibbons

Meet the Author/Illustrator, Gail Gibbons
⭐ Award-winning author ···············➤ 270

Theme Connections ···············➤ 271

Science Inquiry My Grandparents ·······➤ 272

Ants ························➤ 274

poem by Marilyn Singer • *illustrated by* Ken Robbins

Caterpillar ················➤ 276

poem by Christina Rosetti • *illustrated by* Lori Lohstoeter

Test Prep ················➤ 278

Around the Town

Unit Overview ··➤ **282**

Vocabulary Warm-Up ··························➤ **284**

Red Light, Green Light, Mama and Me ·······················➤ **286**
realistic fiction by Cari Best • *illustrated by* Niki Daly

Meet the Author, Cari Best ✦ Award-winning author
Meet the Illustrator, Niki Daly
✦ Award-winning illustrator ··············➤ **310**

Theme Connections ·······················➤ **311**

Social Studies **Inquiry** Saturdays, Mom, and Me ·····➤ **312**

Vocabulary Warm-Up ·······················➤ **314**

In the Money: A Book About Banking ···················➤ **316**
expository text by Nancy Loewen • *illustrated by* Brad Fitzpatrick

Meet the Author, Nancy Loewen
Meet the Illustrator, Brad Fitzpatrick ············➤ **338**

Theme Connections ·······················➤ **339**

Social Studies **Inquiry** Choices ··········➤ **312**

Vocabulary Warm-Up · · · · · · · · · · · · · · · · · ·➤ 342

Jalapeño Bagels · · · · · · · · · · · · · · · ·➤ 344

realistic fiction by Natasha Wing · *illustrated by* Robert Casilla

Meet the Author, Natasha Wing
Meet the Illustrator, Robert Casilla · · · · · · · · · · ·➤ 358

Theme Connections · · · · · · · · · · · · · · · · · ·➤ 359

🌐 **Social Studies** Inquiry Family Tradition · · ·➤ 360

Vocabulary Warm-Up · · · · · · · · · · · · · · · ·➤ 362

Out and About at City Hall · · ·➤ 364

expository text by Nancy Garhan Attebury · *illustrated by* Zachary Trover

Meet the Author, Nancy Garhan Attebury
Meet the Illustrator, Zachary Trover · · · · · · · · ·➤ 384

Theme Connections · · · · · · · · · · · · · ·➤ 385

🌐 **Social Studies** Inquiry Laws · · · · · · · · ·➤ 386

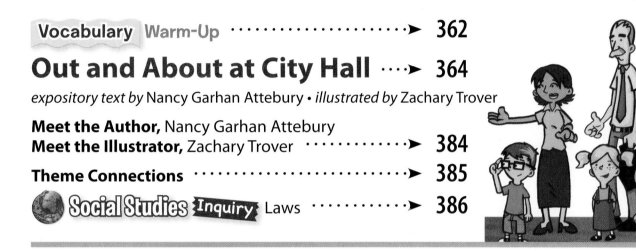

Vocabulary Warm-Up · · · · · · · · · · · · · · · · · ·➤ 388

Grandpa's Corner Store

⭐ Notable Social Studies Trade Book, 2001 · · · · · · · · · · · · ·➤ 390

realistic fiction written and illustrated by DyAnne DiSalvo-Ryan

Meet the Author/Illustrator, DyAnne DiSalvo-Ryan · ·➤ 422

Theme Connections · · · · · · · · · · · · · · · · · ·➤ 423

🌐 **Social Studies** Inquiry How I Get to School · · · · · · · · · ·➤ 424

Supermarket · · · · · · · · · · · · · · · · · ·➤ 426

poem by Lois Lenski · *illustrated by* Joe Cepeda

The Library ·➤ 427

poem by Barbara A. Huff · *illustrated by* Joe Cepeda

Test Prep ·➤ 428

Glossary ·➤ 432

Kindness

What does it mean to be kind? Who is kind? How do you know? Stories can help us learn about kindness.

Theme Connection

Look at the illustration.

- What are the people doing?
- How are they being kind to each other?
- How are they being kind to the earth?

BIG Idea

How can you show kindness to others?

13

Read the article to find the meanings of these words, which are also in "Because of You":

- ✦ feelings
- ✦ share
- ✦ precious
- ✦ care
- ✦ kind

Vocabulary Strategy

A definition is sometimes provided in the text right next to or near the word it is defining. Use **apposition** to find the meanings of *feelings* and *care*.

Vocabulary

Warm-Up

Tia was leaving for camp on Sunday. Her birthday was on Monday. Tia had mixed feelings, or emotions. She was happy to go to camp, but she was sad that she would be away from home on her birthday.

"You will get to share your birthday with precious new friends," said Tia's mother.

Tia was still not sure. "You will not have to care for, or look after, your brother for a whole week," Tia's mother reminded her.

Sunday came too soon. Tia had butterflies in her stomach. Ideas rolled through Tia's head. She hoped the camp leaders would be kind. She hoped she would have fun.

Tia met many other girls at camp. Soon she had many friends.

The week passed quickly. Tia and her friends did many fun things. They made corn-husk dolls. They swam in the lake. They made a bird house.

Tia wrote about her week at camp in her diary. The first page read: *My camp friends made me a birthday cake!*

GAME

Flash Cards
Make a set of flash cards with the vocabulary words. Write the word on one side and its definition on the other side. Use the flash cards to review the vocabulary words and definitions. Then ask a partner to use the cards to quiz you.

Concept Vocabulary

The concept word for this lesson is **thoughtful.** Someone who is *thoughtful* is kind and caring toward other people. How were Tia's friends kind and caring toward her? What are some ways you can be thoughtful?

Genre

Fiction is a made-up story that entertains readers.

Comprehension Strategy

 Making Connections

As you read, make connections between what you know and what you are reading.

Focus Questions

How can you help make the world a kinder place? Why should we be kind to others?

Because of You

by B. G. Hennessy

illustrated by Hiroe Nakata

Each time a child is born,
the world changes.

When you were born, there was a new
person for your family to love and care for.

And because of you, there is one more
person who can love and care for others.

Because of you, there is one more person who will grow and learn and one more person who can teach others.

Because of you, there is one more person to share with.

And there is one more person who can share feelings and ideas, as well as things.

Because of you, there is one more person
who needs help and one more person who
can help others.

When you help, care, share, and listen, you are being kind.

When two people help, care, share, and listen to each other, they are friends.

When people from different countries
help, care, share, and listen to one another,

it is called peace.

Even something as big and important as peace begins with something small and precious.

It might begin . . .

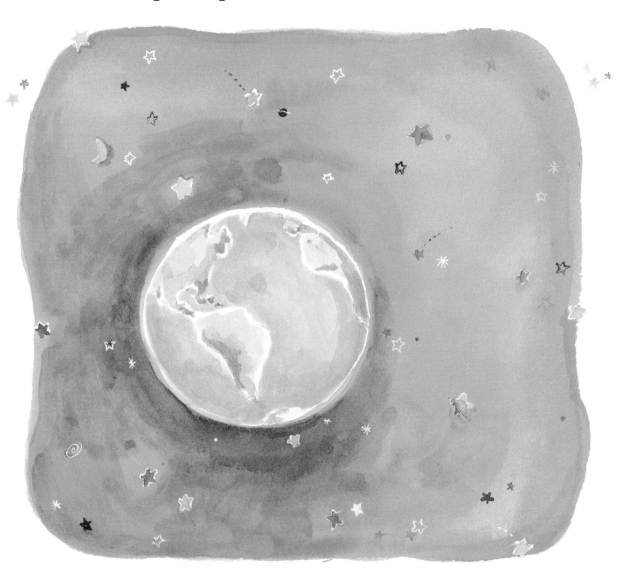

because of you.

Meet the Author

B.G. Hennessy

Hennessy wrote and illustrated her first book when she was just five years old. She says, "Each of us, even the youngest child, makes a difference. Helping children understand that their choices determine what kind of a difference they will make is at the heart of this book."

Meet the Illustrator

Hiroe Nakata

Nakata grew up in Japan. As a child she enjoyed spending time with her grandfather, who was a painter. He encouraged her to paint and sparked her interest in watercolors. At age sixteen, she and her family moved to the United States.

Theme Connections

Within the Selection

1. Why is "Because of You" a good title for this story?

2. How does this story make you feel?

Beyond the Selection

3. What can you do to help someone in your family?

4. How has someone in your family helped you?

5. Think about how "Because of You" adds to what you know about kindness.

Write about It!

Describe a time you shared something with another person.

Remember to look for pictures and articles about kindness to add to the Concept/Question Board.

The Life of Clara Barton

Clara Barton was born in 1821. She began teaching school at age seventeen. By 1845 Barton had founded a public school. She was a teacher there for ten years.

Her ideas to improve the lives of soldiers began in 1861. She knew nurses needed more medical supplies. She began to work hard for this cause.

During the Civil War, Barton was a head nurse. She took care of soldiers. She was also kind to their families. She let them know when their sons were hurt.

In 1881 Clara Barton founded the American National Red Cross. The group did more than help soldiers. They helped people during times of peace as well.

Clara Barton died in 1912. But her kindness is not gone. The American Red Cross still helps people today.

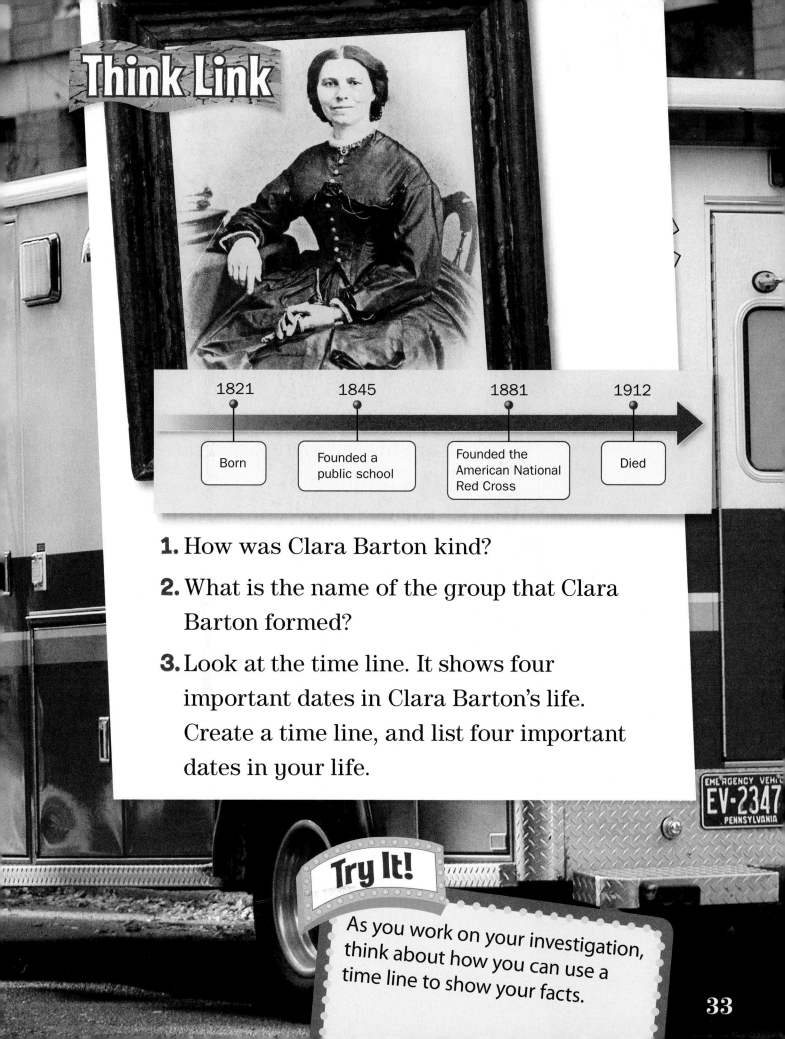

1821 Born
1845 Founded a public school
1881 Founded the American National Red Cross
1912 Died

1. How was Clara Barton kind?

2. What is the name of the group that Clara Barton formed?

3. Look at the time line. It shows four important dates in Clara Barton's life. Create a time line, and list four important dates in your life.

Try It!

As you work on your investigation, think about how you can use a time line to show your facts.

Read the article to find the meanings of these words, which are also in "For the Love of Our Earth":

✦ dawn
✦ engines
✦ glows
✦ witness
✦ litter

Vocabulary Strategy

A definition is sometimes provided in the text right next to or near the word it is defining. Use **apposition** to find the meanings of *glows* and *litter*.

Vocabulary

Warm-Up

It was just after dawn. Ben listened to the engines of the racecars as they sped around the track. Ben had never seen cars move with so much speed.

"The track almost glows, or shines!" Ben shouted to his grandfather.

"Humph!" Ben's grandfather snorted. "It is a needless waste of energy if you ask me."

Ben's uncle patted him on the back. "Your grandfather is from another time," he said. "His ancestors used horses when they wanted to race."

Ben went back to watching the cars.

He was excited to witness his first race.

Ben's grandfather shook his head at all the litter, or trash, he saw. "I do not know what is wrong with people today," he muttered. "When I grew up the air was fresh and clean."

Ben knew why his grandfather was angry. The track had been built where sunflowers once grew. Ben loved the flowers too. In fact, he had saved some of their seeds.

Ben smiled to himself. He had a plan. He would plant the sunflower seeds in his grandfather's yard. "Soon grandfather will smile too," Ben said to himself.

GAME

Guessing Game
Choose a partner. Ask your partner, "What word means 'to see or hear something'?" After correctly guessing *witness*, it is your partner's turn to choose a word for you to guess. Review all the vocabulary words.

Concept Vocabulary

The concept word for this lesson is **respect.** *Respect* means "to be kind and caring toward somebody or something." We can show respect to people, such as our parents and teachers, and to things, such as nature and the environment. How can you show respect to nature or the environment?

Rhyming Fiction is a made-up story that uses rhyme to entertain readers.

Comprehension Strategy

☆ **Summarizing** As you read, use your own words to sum up the important points and information in the story.

For the Love of Our Earth

by P.K. Hallinan

Focus Questions

In what ways can we show kindness to our earth?

Why is being kind to our earth important?

For the love of our earth,
we'll clean up the land.
We'll pick up the litter.
We'll sift through the sand.

For the love of our earth,
we'll nurture new trees.
We'll bring back the flowers.
We'll bring back the seas.

We'll clean all the rivers, the lakes, and the streams till pure water shimmers like radiant beams.

Then taking ahold of the
work to be done,
we'll lighten the sky and
we'll brighten the sun.

For the love of our earth,
we'll try to renew
the bountiful garden
our ancestors knew.

We'll harvest our crops
to help feed the poor.
We'll share what we have,
so that all can have more.

Yes, we'll slowly return
to our original place
as children of nature
in its infinite grace.

And then as one family,
we'll witness the birth
of peace everlasting . . .

for the love of our earth.

Meet the Author and Illustrator

P.K. Hallinan

Hallinan began writing and illustrating thirty-five years ago when he created a picture book for his two young sons. Since then he has written more than eighty children's books. *For the Love of Our Earth* was recognized by Early Childhood News as one of America's "100 Best Product Picks for Children."

Kindness

Theme Connections

Within the Selection

1. What are some ways you can be kind to our earth?

2. What does the story tell us we will do after we harvest the crops?

Across Selections

3. How is "For the Love of Our Earth" like "Because of You"?

4. How are the two stories different?

Beyond the Selection

5. Why should we be kind to our earth?

6. Think about how "For the Love of Our Earth" adds to what you know about kindness.

Write about It!

Make a list of three ways you can be kind to our earth.

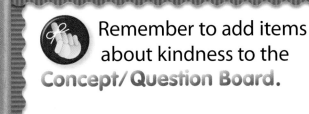

Remember to add items about kindness to the Concept/Question Board.

Genre

Newspaper Articles tell about people, places, or things that happen in nations, states, and cities.

Feature

Bylines tell who wrote the article.

Schools to Celebrate Earth Day

by Aaron Peres

Earth Day is celebrated every year on April 22. It is a special day to take care of Earth. Schools in our area will celebrate in many ways.

Maria Del is a student at Forest Elementary School. "My class is going to reuse cans," she said. "We are going to bring in used cans and make pencil holders out of them!"

Apple Elementary School students will collect rain water. Celia Jenkins is in the second grade there. "My whole class is going to collect rain water," she said. "We are going to put buckets outside, under the gutters. Then we can reuse the water for plants."

The mayor is proud of the students. "I am glad students are recycling and helping to save water, a natural resource. I hope other people will witness these good activities and celebrate Earth Day."

Think Link

1. Who wrote the newspaper article?

2. Why might someone consider collecting rain water?

3. What are some ways students in the article are helping Earth?

Try It!

As you work on your investigation, remember to look in newspaper articles for information.

Read the article to find the meanings of these words, which are also in "The Elves and the Shoemaker":

✦ elves
✦ shoemaker
✦ flash
✦ leather
✦ finest

Vocabulary Strategy

A definition is sometimes provided in the text right next to or near the word it is defining. Use **apposition** to find the meanings of *flash* and *finest*.

Vocabulary
Warm-Up

A group of elves gathered under the old oak tree in the woods. "I have spent my entire life as a shoemaker," said one elf.

"So have I," said another. "But we never get to see people wearing our shoes."

"We should take a trip to the city!" said the first elf.

In a flash, or instant, the elves went to the city. They were happy to see people wearing their shoes.

The next day, the elves returned to the woods. They did their regular work.

The first elf cut a piece of leather. He thought as he cut.

"I want to make my shoes better. I want to make the finest, or best, shoes," he said. "I need someone to do the sewing. I need someone who will not miss a stitch!"

"I can do that!" said an elf with a hurt foot. "I can sit down and sew all day!"

"I need someone to knit too," said the shoemaker. "I want to make socks to go with each pair of shoes."

"I can knit!" said one elf.

"So can I," said another.

From that day, the elves lived peacefully in the woods. They made the finest shoes and socks.

GAME

Draw
Illustrate the story you just read. Put as many vocabulary words as you can in your picture. Write the vocabulary words that are not in your picture at the bottom of your illustration.

Concept Vocabulary

The concept word for this lesson is **helpful.** *Helpful* means "providing or willing to provide assistance, information, or other aid." The elves were being helpful when they offered to sew and knit for the other elf. How can you be helpful to members of your family?

Genre

A **fairy tale** is a story that involves imaginary creatures with magical powers, mysterious adventures or occurrences, and a happy ending.

Comprehension Skill

☆ **Sequence**
As you read, pay attention to the order in which the events in the story take place.

Focus Questions

Is it better to give kindness or to receive it? How does being kind to others make you feel?

The Elves and the Shoemaker

by Brothers Grimm
retold by Emily Greggs and
Bethany Martin
illustrated by Viktor Shatunov

Once upon a time there lived a shoemaker. He worked very hard, but he was still very poor.

At last he had only one piece of leather. It was just enough to make one pair of shoes.

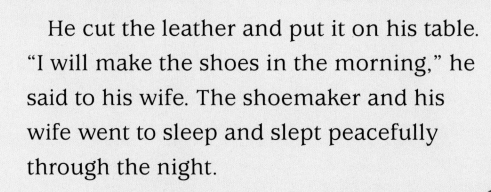

He cut the leather and put it on his table. "I will make the shoes in the morning," he said to his wife. The shoemaker and his wife went to sleep and slept peacefully through the night.

In the morning he went to his table. To his
amazement, the shoes were already made.
The shoemaker did not know what to think.
They were the finest shoes he had ever seen.

The same day a rich man came into the shop. "I like these shoes very much. They are just my size," said the man. "I will pay you a higher price than usual for them." And he gave the shoemaker two coins.

The shoemaker used the two coins to buy leather for two more pairs of shoes. He cut the leather and went to bed.

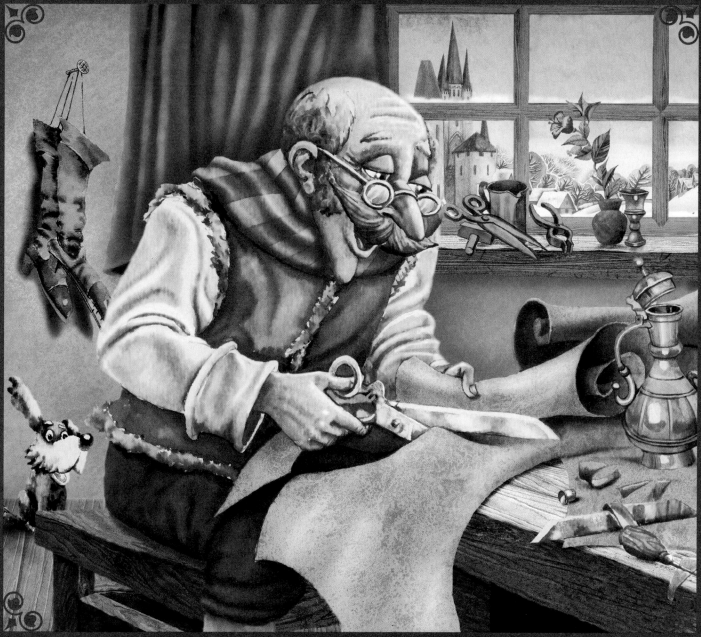

In the morning the shoemaker found two pairs of shoes already made. "Who is making these shoes?" said the shoemaker. "These are the best shoes I have ever seen."

Soon two customers came in and bought the shoes. They paid him four coins. The shoemaker bought leather for four more pairs of shoes.

Just as before, he cut out the leather. In the morning he found four more pairs of shoes. Soon four customers came in and bought the shoes. And so it went for some time.

"I would like to stay up tonight to see who is making the shoes," said the shoemaker. His wife liked the idea too. So they hid behind a curtain. They watched and waited.

At midnight in came two little elves. They sat on the table and went right to work. They stitched and sewed. The elves worked until all the shoes were done. Then they were gone in a flash.

The next day the wife said, "These elves have been so kind to us. I want to do something kind for them. They need new clothes to keep warm. I will make each of them pants, a shirt, and a coat. And you can make them each a pair of shoes." And they went right to work.

One night the shoemaker did not leave leather on the table. He left the nice clothes and shoes instead. The shoemaker and his wife hid behind the curtain to see what the elves would do.

At midnight in came the two little elves. When they saw the clothes for them, they laughed and hopped around the room. "Look how happy they are!" the shoemaker whispered to his wife.

The elves put on the clothes and skipped and danced. At last they danced out the door and were never seen again.

And the kind shoemaker and his wife lived happily ever after.

Meet the Authors

Brothers Grimm

The Brothers Grimm were Jacob and Wilhelm Grimm who were born in Germany in 1785 (Jacob) and 1786 (Wilhelm). They spent years collecting and researching folktales and fairy tales. They published many collections of some of the world's most famous stories, including *Cinderella, Hansel and Gretel,* and *Rumpelstiltskin.*

Meet the Illustrator

Viktor Shatunov

Shatunov is Russian, but he currently lives in Lithuania. He thinks fairy tales and folk tales are the most interesting types of stories to illustrate because he is able to create something new.

Theme Connections

Within the Selection

1. How did the elves show kindness?

2. How did the shoemaker and his wife show kindness?

Across Selections

3. How are the elves similar to the people in "For the Love of Our Earth"?

Beyond the Selection

4. Have you ever returned kindness to someone who was kind to you? What did you do?

5. Think about how "The Elves and the Shoemaker" adds to what you know about kindness.

Write about It!

Describe a time when you were kind to someone. Did they return your kindness?

Remember to add items about kindness to the **Concept/Question Board.**

Trade

Trade has been around for many years. Long ago pioneers trapped animals. They traded fur for food. Trade was a way of life. It was a way to survive.

Trade is still used today. There are even clubs for people who trade. People in these clubs make lists. The lists name skills and items that can be traded. The lists might include food, clothing, or yard work. People can even trade knowledge.

Everyone has a skill or a talent. Some people are good at cooking. Some people are good at sewing. A good cook might need a button sewn on a shirt. A sewer might not know how to cook dinner. These two people could trade their skills and help each other.

People in different countries trade too. A family in Mexico might trade goods with a family in Ohio. Then both families help each other and get what they need.

Trading is a way to get things. You do not need money to trade. It can be a good way to make new friends or help old friends.

Think Link

1. Look at the third paragraph. Why do you think the word *everyone* is in bold print?

2. Why might a family in Ohio trade with a family in Mexico?

3. Why do you think the pioneers traded?

Try It!

As you work on your investigation, think about using bold text to emphasize certain words.

THE LION
AND
THE MOUSE

by Michael Morpurgo
from *The McElderry Book of Aesop's Fables*
illustrated by Emma Chichester Clark

Read the article to find the meanings of these words, which are also in "The Lion and the Mouse":

✦ snoozing
✦ furious
✦ repay
✦ raged
✦ gnaw

Vocabulary Strategy

Context Clues in the text help you find the meanings of words. Use context clues to find the meanings of *snoozing* and *gnaw*.

Vocabulary

Warm-Up

I saw my cat snoozing in the sunshine. A thought flashed through my mind. Just the other day I had seen Sophie stalking a chipmunk in the garden. I was furious! "We should bring her inside!" I said. "I do not want her to harm any chipmunks!"

Gran agreed. "Bring her in if it makes you feel better, Toby," she said. "Do not be mad at Sophie though. Chasing chipmunks is what makes Sophie a cat!"

Gran is kind. She shows her kindness by taking the time to explain things to me. I repay her kindness by listening closely to what she says. "Think about the cats in the wild," Gran explained. "Lions sleep during the day. Then they hunt smaller animals at dusk."

My mind saw the chipmunk as it ran away. "Stop, Gran!" I raged. "I do not want to hear about lions. I do not even like to see dogs gnaw on bones!"

But Gran did not stop. "Nature has a beautiful way of taking care of things," she said. "Big animals eat smaller animals. Some animals eat insects, and that is good too!"

GAME

Matching Game
Write each vocabulary word on an index card. Then write each word's meaning on its own card. Turn over and spread out the cards. Take turns with a partner matching each word with its meaning.

Concept Vocabulary

The concept word for this lesson is **sympathy.** *Sympathy* is "the ability to feel and understand the sorrow or troubles of others." We can show sympathy toward a sick friend or a hurt animal. What have you done to show sympathy toward a friend?

Genre

A **fable** is a short story that teaches a lesson or moral.

Comprehension Skill

 Reality and Fantasy

As you read, identify the things and events in the story that are real and the things and events that are make-believe.

Focus Questions

Can animals be kind to one another? In what ways do you think animals can show kindness?

THE LION

AND

THE MOUSE

by Michael Morpurgo

from *The McElderry Book of Aesop's Fables*

illustrated by Emma Chichester Clark

One hot afternoon, Lion lay snoozing
happily in the shade of a tree. Suddenly
he felt something running over his nose.
He opened one eye and saw it was a
tiny mouse. Furious at being woken, he
waited his moment—then he flashed
out his great paw and caught Mouse by
the tail.

"Oh, please," squeaked Mouse, "I didn't mean to wake you. Let me go, please. I'll pay you back one day, I promise."

Lion roared with laughter, "You repay me? A little tiddly thing like you! How could such a puny creature be of any use to a king of the beasts like me?"

"Please, great King," cried Mouse, "don't eat me." Lion yawned and thought about it. He was too sleepy.

"Oh well. If you insist. After all, you wouldn't make much of a meal, would you? Off you go, and be careful whose nose you walk on in the future."

It was not long after that Mouse and Lion met again. This is how it happened. Lion had gone off hunting at dusk. He was stalking through the trees, following a herd of zebra, when he happened to spring a hunter's trap. A great net came down on him and held him fast. He roared and raged, but in spite of all his great strength, he could not break free. His roaring echoed through the forest so that everyone heard him and everyone knew that Lion was in trouble.

Mouse heard him too, and he was a
mouse of his word. Off he went, as fast
as his little legs would carry him, to see
if he could help. It wasn't long before he
came across Lion still caught up
in the net, still roaring and raging.
"Don't worry," said Mouse.
"I'll soon have you out of that."
And he began to gnaw at the
net ropes one by one, until
at last Lion could break free.

"There you are," said Mouse. "I told you I'd pay you back, didn't I?"

"A little tiddly thing like you helping out a king of the beasts like me," Lion replied. "Who'd have thought it possible?"

"Everything is possible," said Mouse. "Good-bye, Lion." And off he scampered, away into the long grass.

KINDNESS IS MORE IMPORTANT THAN STRENGTH.

Meet the Author

Michael Morpurgo

Morpurgo has written over ninety-five books and has won numerous awards, including the Smarties Prize and the Children's Book Award. He enjoys farm life and runs a charity to help children from the city experience the fun of country living.

Meet the Illustrator

Emma Chichester Clark

Clark was born in London but lived in Ireland for most of her childhood. She has illustrated more than forty collections and picture books and has won many awards, including the Mother Goose Award.

Theme Connections

Within the Selection

1. Why do you think Lion let Mouse go?

2. How did Mouse repay Lion's kindness?

Across Selections

3. How is Mouse in "The Lion and the Mouse" like the shoemaker and his wife in "The Elves and the Shoemaker"?

Beyond the Selection

4. What does "Kindness is more important than strength" mean?

5. Think about how "The Lion and the Mouse" adds to what you know about kindness.

Write about It!

Pretend you are an animal. How would you be kind to other animals?

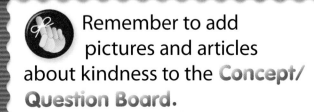

Remember to add pictures and articles about kindness to the Concept/Question Board.

SURVIVAL

Some animals eat other animals. Lions like to stalk other animals. Then the lion attacks.

Some animals eat plants. Cows and horses eat grass. These animals depend on plants for food.

Some animals help plants. Giraffes eat leaves from branches high in trees. With the leaves gone, more sunlight can reach the ground. Plants on the ground grow faster.

Animals are not the only ones who use plants. People use plants and trees for many different things. Did you know that some medicines are made from trees and plants? Plants also make oxygen. People and animals need oxygen to breathe.

In this cycle of life, plants and animals need each other.

This lion is hungry. It is stalking another animal.

1. How did the caption help you understand the photo?

2. How do giraffes help plants on the ground to grow?

3. What are some ways people use plants?

Try It!

As you work on your investigation, remember to use captions to describe your photos.

Read the article to find the meanings of these words, which are also in "Corduroy":

- palace
- escalator
- dashing
- yanked
- fastened

Vocabulary Strategy

Context Clues in the text help you find the meanings of words. Use context clues to find the meanings of *palace, yanked,* and *fastened.*

Vocabulary
Warm-Up

Maria looked around the store. There were all kinds of things that would look good in her bedroom. "I want my room to be fancy. I want it to look like a palace," she said to her mother. "I have saved fifty dollars, but I do not want to spend it all at once."

Maria's mother pointed to the escalator. "We should try downstairs. That is where the sale items are."

"That is a great idea," said Maria as she began dashing toward the escalator.

A beaded lamp caught Maria's eye. Maria pulled

and yanked the lamp off the shelf. "Be careful, Maria!" said her mother. "Calm down, and see how much it costs."

The lamp cost fifteen dollars. Maria bought the lamp. She found a golden bedspread. It cost fifteen dollars too. "You have some money left," said Maria's mother. "How will you spend it?"

Maria fastened the last button on her coat. "Let me look at my list," she said. "Can we stop by the paint store? I want to paint my palace royal blue!" laughed Maria. "Thanks for taking me shopping today, Mom. This has been a great day!"

Fill In the Blank
On a sheet of paper, use each of the vocabulary words in a sentence. Draw a blank line in place of each vocabulary word. Give your paper to another student. Have your partner fill in each blank with the correct vocabulary word.

Concept Vocabulary

The concept word for this lesson is **grateful**. *Grateful* means "full of thanks for a favor or for something that makes you happy." Maria thanked her mother for taking her shopping. Why should we tell someone we are grateful for something they have done?

Fantasy is a story that could not happen in the real world.

Making Inferences

As you read, use the information in the text and your own knowledge to make inferences about the characters or the events in the story.

Corduroy

by Don Freeman

Focus Questions

How can being kind help you make friends? Should kindness be determined by outward appearances?

Corduroy is a bear who once lived in the toy department of a big store. Day after day he waited with all the other animals and dolls for someone to come along and take him home.

The store was always filled with shoppers buying all sorts of things, but no one ever seemed to want a small bear in green overalls.

Then one morning a little girl stopped and looked straight into Corduroy's bright eyes.

"Oh, Mommy!" she said. "Look! There's the very bear I've always wanted."

"Not today, dear." Her mother sighed. "I've spent too much already. Besides, he doesn't look new. He's lost the button to one of his shoulder straps."

Corduroy watched them sadly as they walked away.

"I didn't know I'd lost a button," he said to himself. "Tonight I'll go and see if I can find it."

Late that evening, when all the shoppers had gone and the doors were shut and locked, Corduroy climbed carefully down from his shelf and began searching everywhere on the floor for his lost button.

Suddenly he felt the floor moving under him! Quite by accident he had stepped onto an escalator—and up he went!

"Could this be a mountain?" he wondered. "I think I've always wanted to climb a mountain."

He stepped off the escalator as it reached the next floor, and there, before his eyes, was a most amazing sight—tables and chairs and lamps and sofas, and rows and rows of beds. "This must be a palace!" Corduroy gasped. "I guess I've always wanted to live in a palace."

He wandered around admiring the furniture.

"This must be a bed," he said. "I've always wanted to sleep in a bed." And up he crawled onto a large, thick mattress.

All at once he saw something small and round.

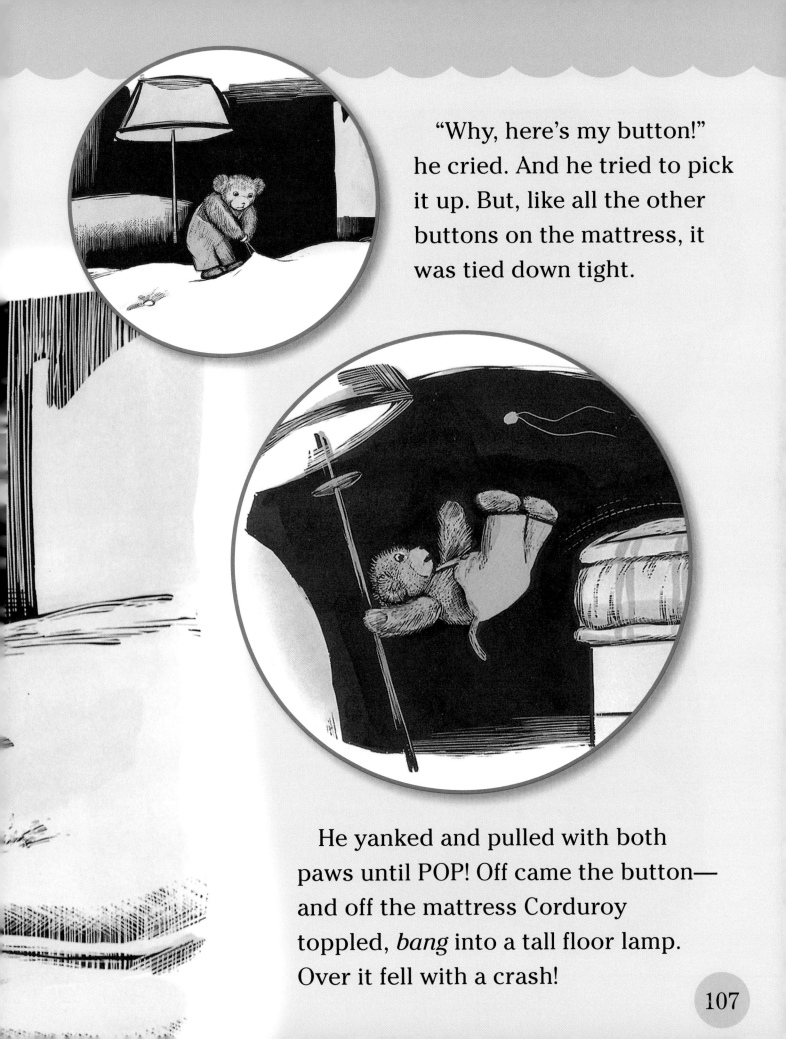

"Why, here's my button!" he cried. And he tried to pick it up. But, like all the other buttons on the mattress, it was tied down tight.

He yanked and pulled with both paws until POP! Off came the button—and off the mattress Corduroy toppled, *bang* into a tall floor lamp. Over it fell with a crash!

Corduroy didn't
know it, but there was
someone else awake
in the store. The night
watchman was going
his rounds on the
floor above. When he
heard the crash he
came dashing down
the escalator.

"Now who in the world did that!" he exclaimed. "Somebody must be hiding around here!"

He flashed his light under and over sofas and beds until he came to the biggest bed of all. And there he saw two fuzzy brown ears sticking up from under the cover.

"Hello!" he said. "How did *you* get upstairs?"

The watchman
tucked Corduroy
under his arm and carried
him down the escalator and
set him on the shelf in the toy
department with the other
animals and dolls.

Corduroy was just waking up when the first customers came into the store in the morning. And there, looking at him with a wide, warm smile, was the same little girl he'd seen only the day before.

"I'm Lisa," she said, "and you're going to be my very own bear. Last night I counted what I've saved in my piggy bank and my mother said I could bring you home."

"Shall I put him in a box for you?" the saleslady asked.

"Oh, no thank you," Lisa answered. And she carried Corduroy home in her arms.

She ran all the way up four flights of stairs, into her family's apartment, and straight to her own room.

Corduroy blinked. There was a chair and a chest of drawers, and alongside a girl-size bed stood a little bed just the right size for him. The room was small, nothing like that enormous palace in the department store.

"This must be home," he said. "I *know* I've always wanted a home!"

Lisa sat down with Corduroy on her lap
and began to sew a button on his overalls.

"I like you the way you are," she said,
"but you'll be more comfortable with your
shoulder strap fastened."

"You must be a friend," said Corduroy. "I've always wanted a friend."

"Me too!" said Lisa, and gave him a big hug.

Meet the Author and Illustrator

Don Freeman

Freeman had a job playing the trumpet until he left his trumpet on the subway in New York City. He forgot his trumpet because he was so busy drawing for his art class. From then on, Freeman made his living drawing pictures. Freeman wrote and illustrated his first children's book for his young son, Roy. Many more books followed, including *Corduroy*.

Theme Connections

Within the Selection

1. How was Lisa kind to Corduroy?

2. Who else was kind to Corduroy?

Across Selections

3. How was Lisa's kindness to Corduroy similar to the kindness the shoemaker and his wife showed to the elves?

Beyond the Selection

4. Would you choose a bear like Corduroy if you saw him in a store? Why or why not?

5. Think about how "Corduroy" adds to what you know about kindness.

Write about It!

Describe your favorite stuffed animal or toy.

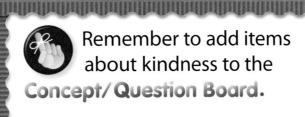

Remember to add items about kindness to the Concept/Question Board.

Lunch Money

Brandon was sitting under a tree. He looked sad.

"Hi, Brandon. What is wrong?" I asked.

"I forgot my lunch money," said Brandon. "Now I cannot eat lunch."

I thought about what I could do to help him. That day was my favorite day of the week for lunch. It was chicken and green beans day. "How much money do you need?" I asked.

"I need two dollars for a piece of chicken," he said.

I thought about it. "I have three dollars," I said. "Chicken with green beans costs three dollars. But if I buy only chicken, I can give one dollar to you."

"Would you do that for me?" Brandon asked. "Would you give up having green beans today?"

"Of course I would!" I exclaimed. "After all, you are my friend."

"Ramón, would you give up having green beans today and give Brandon one dollar?" I asked. "He forgot his lunch money. I am giving him one dollar."

"Sure I would!" Ramón said. "We should go eat lunch now. I am hungry!"

Think Link

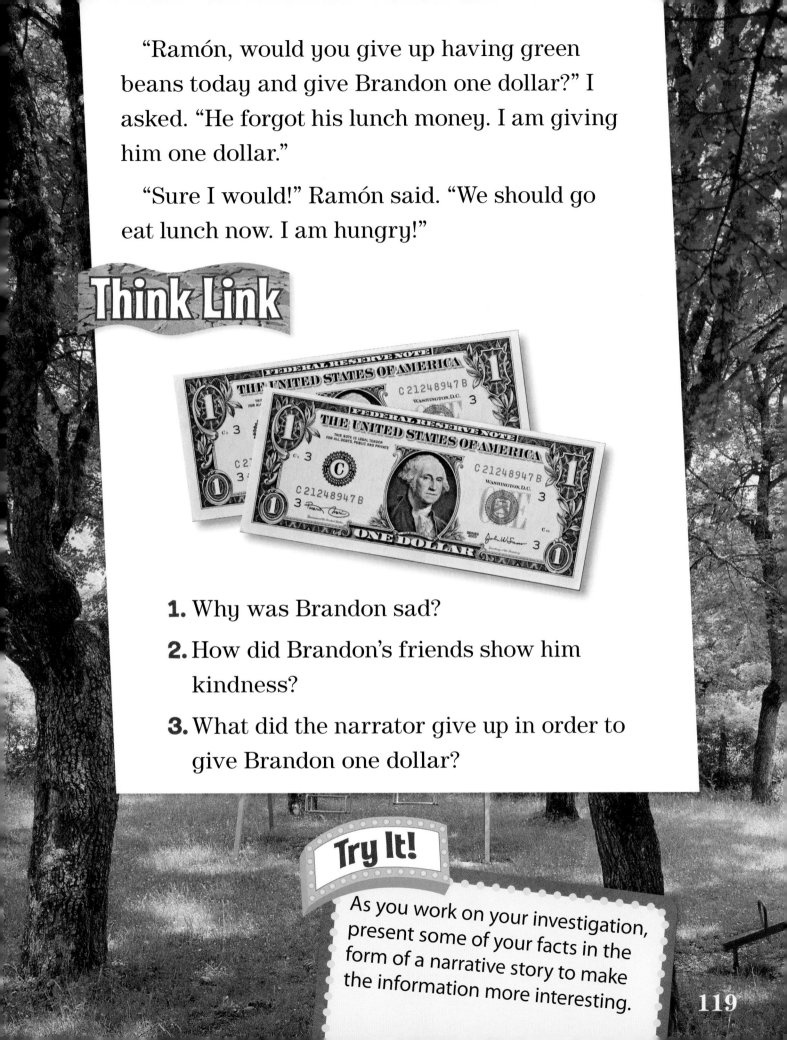

1. Why was Brandon sad?

2. How did Brandon's friends show him kindness?

3. What did the narrator give up in order to give Brandon one dollar?

Try It!

As you work on your investigation, present some of your facts in the form of a narrative story to make the information more interesting.

dear tulips

by Takayo Noda

you are
red
yellow
orange
just like my lollipops

please fill
my whole house
today
because my mother
is not feeling well

you will
make her better
for she loves
flowers

please tell me
that you'll come

120

Focus Questions What kind things does your family do for you when you are sick? What do you do for your family members when one of them is sick?

Sick Days

by Mary Ann Hoberman

illustrated by Marylin Hafner

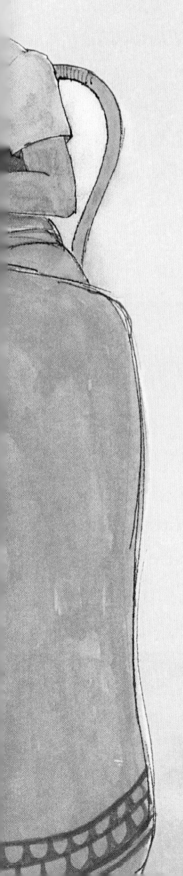

On days when I am sick in bed

My mother is so nice;

She brings me bowls of chicken soup

And ginger ale with ice.

She cuts the crusts off buttered toast

And serves it on a tray

And sits down while I eat it

And doesn't go away.

She reads my favorite books to me;

She lets me take my pick;

And everything is perfect—

Except that I am sick!

Test Prep

Test-Taking Strategy: Listening Carefully

When you take a test, listen carefully so you know what you are supposed to do. You will have to answer different kinds of questions on a test. Listening carefully will help you choose the correct answers.

Listening Carefully

Listen carefully to the directions for this question.

> **EXAMPLE**
>
> **1.** Look at the three words below. Which word has the same MIDDLE sound as *red*?
>   ○ met
>   ○ rat
>   ○ bad

The first answer is correct because it has the same MIDDLE sound as *red*. If you did not listen carefully, you might have chosen one of the other answers. One has the same beginning sound as *red*, and the other has the same ending sound as *red*.

A Helpful Idea

Emily and her family lived next to Miss Joan. She was an older woman who had no family nearby. Miss Joan had two dogs and a horse. She liked to ride her horse and walk her dogs. Sometimes she got tired and could not spend time with her animals.

Emily and her brother, Marco, talked to their parents about helping Miss Joan. Mr. and Mrs. Hoffman said it was a wonderful idea. They just had to do it in a nice way.

"How about this?" asked Marco. "We will ask her if we can help." Everybody thought this was a good idea.

GO ON

The next morning, Emily visited her neighbor. "Miss Joan, I have a favor to ask. Can I help take care of Boots?" Emily petted the horse as she spoke.

"Why, of course," said Miss Joan. "Boots just loves you. He would be happy to see more of you."

Emily had asked about Boots. Now Marco would ask about the dogs. He knew exactly what he would do.

In the afternoon, Marco visited Miss Joan. "Can I take Ginger and Sasha for a walk, Miss Joan? I want to see if the owls are still near the nest."

"That would be wonderful. I am feeling a little tired. I know the dogs would love to go for a walk. Thank you so much, Marco," Miss Joan said. "You and Emily are such a big help. I know Boots, Sasha, and Ginger are as grateful as I am."

1. This story is probably a _____.

  ○ fable

  ○ poem

  ○ true story

  ○ fairy tale

2. What is the name of the horse in the story?

  ○ Wonder

  ○ Boots

  ○ Ginger

  ○ Sasha

3. The story does <u>not</u> tell _____.

  ○ where Marco wanted to walk

  ○ who had the good idea

  ○ the names of the dogs

  ○ what type of dogs Miss Joan has

4. Whom does Miss Joan say the last sentence to?

  ○ Marco

  ○ Emily

  ○ Mr. Hoffman

  ○ Mrs. Hoffman

5. If you do not know what *grateful* means, you should _____.

  ○ think about the sentence that it is a part of

  ○ look for other things Miss Joan said

  ○ spell it to yourself

  ○ skip over the word

STOP

Let's Explore

Go outside. Look around. What do you see? Do you see trees or dirt? Do you see bugs, birds, or rocks? Explore the outdoors, and discover the natural world around you.

Theme Connection

Look at the photograph.

- What do you see?
- What is the girl doing?
- How does this photograph relate to the theme Let's Explore?

BIG Idea

What did you discover outside today?

Read the article to find the meanings of these words, which are also in "Ants! They are hard workers!":

✦ insects
✦ cocoon
✦ tunnels
✦ enemies
✦ invade

Vocabulary Strategy

Context Clues in the text help you find the meanings of words. Use context clues to find the meanings of *insects* and *enemies*.

Vocabulary

Warm-Up

I love insects. Insects fascinate me. They do not fascinate my sister. She does not like bugs!

I have tried everything to make my sister understand. I have shown my sister silky spider webs. I think they are beautiful, but she does not. My sister saw a cocoon the other day. "Bagworms are going to come out of there," she groaned.

I got out my book about insects. I showed my sister tunnels that

ants make. "Ants work very hard," I said to my sister.

"They ruin picnics," she exclaimed. "Ants are my enemies!" My sister went back to her art project.

"Bugs are very interesting," I said. "Do you know that some ants squirt poison from their mouths?"

My sister was not impressed. She told me not to invade her space. *Let her have her art project,* I thought to myself. *I have my insects!*

GAME

Guessing Game
Choose a partner. Ask your partner, "What word means 'to enter without an invitation'?" After correctly guessing *invade*, it is your partner's turn to choose a word for you to guess. Review all the vocabulary words.

Concept Vocabulary

The concept word for this lesson is ***research.*** *Research* means "to study carefully to find and learn facts." You can use books, magazines, encyclopedias, and the Internet to help you research topics. What are some topics you would like to research?

Genre

Expository Text is written to inform or explain. It contains facts about real people, things, or events.

Comprehension Skill

☆ **Author's Purpose**

As you read, determine whether the author wrote the story to entertain, to persuade, or to inform the reader.

ANTS!
They are hard workers!

by the Editors of TIME For Kids
with Brenda Iasevoli

Focus Questions

Have you ever found ants in your backyard? How much do you know about the daily lives of ants?

The Ants Go Marching

Citronella ants

An army of ants is hard at work.

Ants are busy digging.

They are crawling on the ground.

They are searching for food.

Ants are insects.

Like all insects, they have six legs
and three body parts.

They have a hard covering, much like a shell.

Here are the parts of a queen ant.

Wings
Only queens and male
ants have wings. These
ants fly up into the sky
to mate.

Abdomen
The abdomen holds the
organs. It is also where
ants store food.

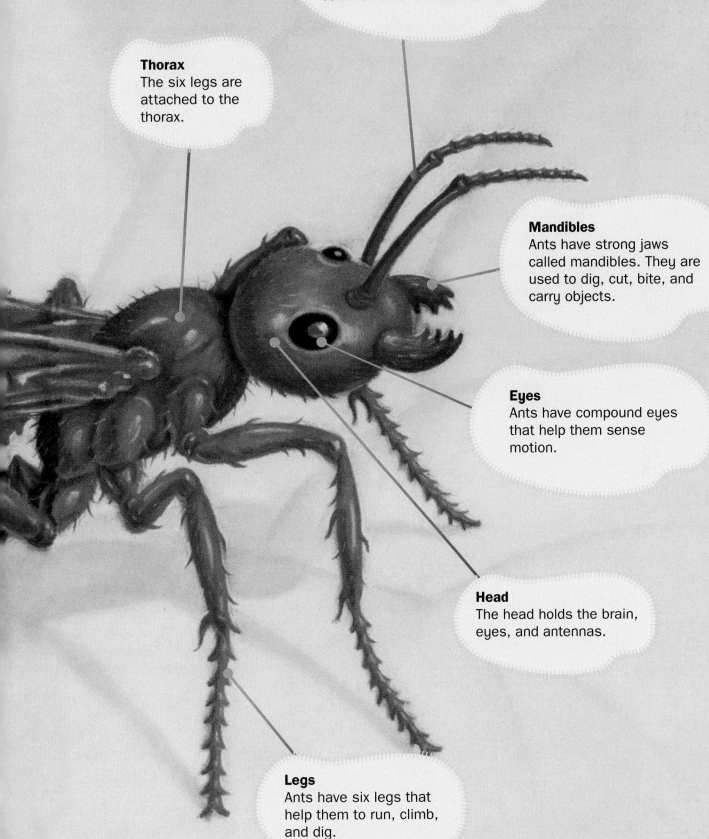

Antennas
These feelers help ants to touch, taste, and smell. Ants also use their antennas to communicate with each other.

Thorax
The six legs are attached to the thorax.

Mandibles
Ants have strong jaws called mandibles. They are used to dig, cut, bite, and carry objects.

Eyes
Ants have compound eyes that help them sense motion.

Head
The head holds the brain, eyes, and antennas.

Legs
Ants have six legs that help them to run, climb, and dig.

137

How Big?

The atomic ant is the smallest ant. It is about the size of a grain of sand!

The giant tropical hunting ant is the biggest ant. It can grow to be more than one and one-half inches long!

There are nearly twelve thousand different kinds of ants.

They can be brown, green, black, red, yellow, purple, or blue.

Ants live everywhere except Antarctica.

Green head ants

139

All in the Family

A queen ant and workers

Most ants live in groups called colonies.

A colony has three types of ants: queens, males, and workers.

Queens have two important jobs.

They mate with male ants and lay eggs.

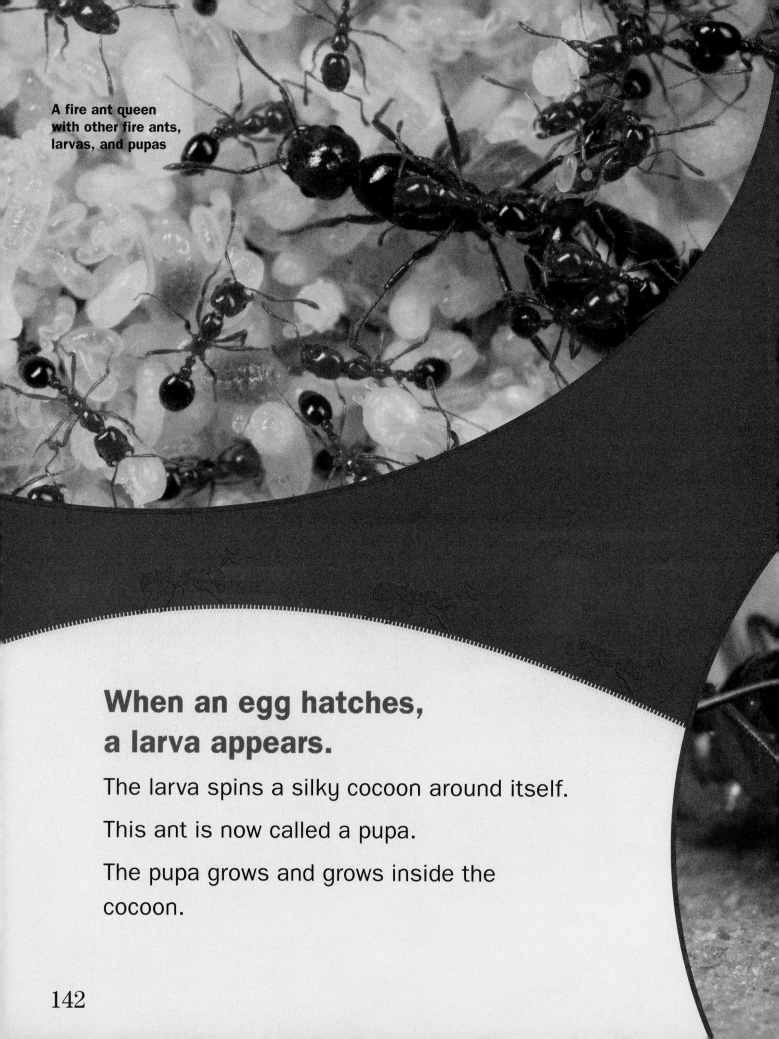

A fire ant queen with other fire ants, larvas, and pupas

When an egg hatches, a larva appears.

The larva spins a silky cocoon around itself.

This ant is now called a pupa.

The pupa grows and grows inside the cocoon.

142

Worker ants bite open the cocoon.

The grown ant comes out!

Workers take care of the queen and younger ants.

They also protect the colony.

Spotted sugar worker ants with cocoons

Ant homes are called nests.

Most ants build their nests under ground.

They dig tunnels and rooms.

They carry the extra dirt outside.

It forms an anthill.

A harvester
ant anthill

144

Weaver ants build their nests in trees.

Some ants hold the edges of leaves.

Other workers carry larvas along the edges.

Larva silk glues the leaves together.

145

Snack Attack!

A harvester ant with a seed

Ants eat both plants and animals.

They look for seeds, fruit, bread, and even other insects.

Ants carry food back to the colony to share.

Some honey pot ants store a juice called honeydew.

When a honey pot ant is hungry, it taps its antennas on a fat ant.

The fat honey pot ant spits honeydew into the mouth of the hungry ant.

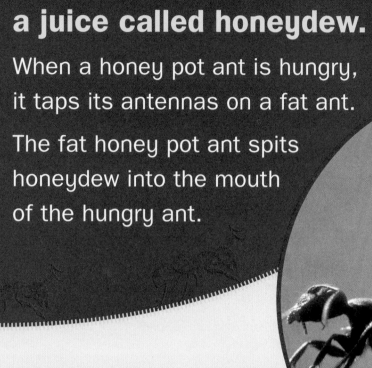

Honey pot ants

Leaf cutter ants are farmers.

They cut and chew leaves with their sharp mandibles.

Then they make a paste.

The paste is used to grow a garden.

Leaf cutter ants

Ants and Enemies

A bee killer bug
and a tiny ant

Ants have many enemies.

Spiders, birds, lizards, anteaters, and other animals eat ants.

But ants will fight to protect themselves and their colony.

151

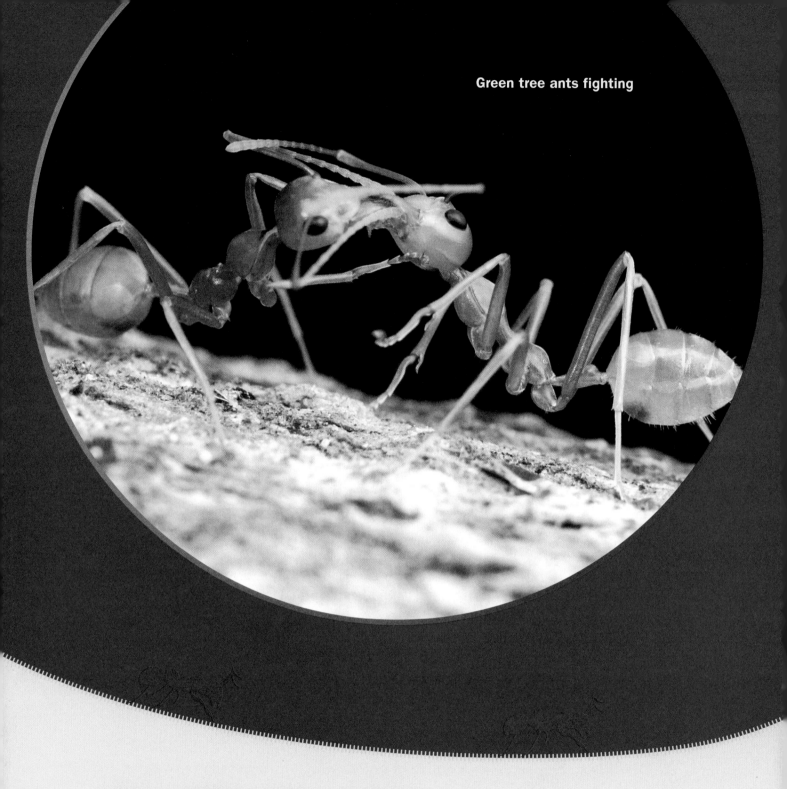

Green tree ants fighting

Ants fight each other.

They use their mandibles to bite.

Some ants squirt poison from their mouths into their enemies.

Ants have been on the earth for millions of years.

Giant dinosaurs disappeared.

But tiny ants survived.

Remember that the next time ants invade your picnic!

Ants from Kenya

153

Brenda Iasevoli

Iasevoli did not realize she wanted to be a writer until she was an adult. During her teaching career, Iasevoli published a school newspaper with her fourth-grade students. This helped her develop an interest for news and information. She likes to write and edit nonfiction books and articles because she likes to learn about new things. Writing does not always come easily for her. When she has difficulty starting, she brainstorms ideas, just as she used to teach her fourth-grade students to do.

Theme Connections

Within the Selection

1. How do you know an ant is an insect?

2. Do you think ants are hard workers? Why or why not?

Beyond the Selection

3. What other bugs live underground?

4. Think about how "Ants! They are hard workers!" adds to what you know about the theme Let's Explore.

Write about It!

Pretend you are an ant. Describe what your day might be like.

Remember to look for pictures and articles about ants and other insects to add to the Concept/Question Board.

Science Inquiry

From Eggs to Butterflies

Butterflies do not always look like butterflies. They have many life stages.

First a butterfly begins as a tiny egg. Inside the egg, a larva forms. It comes out as a caterpillar.

A caterpillar eats all the time. It mainly eats leaves. It eats for almost two weeks. The caterpillar grows and grows. Its skin gets tight. Then it sheds its skin so new, bigger skin can grow.

One day, the caterpillar stops growing. It attaches itself to a twig. Then it splits open to lose its skin for the last time. Now the caterpillar is a pupa.

The pupa becomes a butterfly. Its body is curled and wet. It has to stretch its body and dry its wings.

Finally the butterfly looks like its mother. It flies away to begin this final stage of its life.

Think Link

1. List three sequence words found in this article.

2. Why does a caterpillar shed its skin?

3. Using sequence words, explain how a caterpillar changes into a butterfly.

Try It!

As you work on your investigation, remember to use sequence words when you are describing a sequence of events.

Read the article to find the meanings of these words, which are also in "If You Find a Rock":

- chain
- trace
- fossil
- print
- outstretched

Vocabulary Strategy

Context Clues in the text help you find the meanings of words. Use context clues to find the meanings of *trace, fossil,* and *outstretched.*

Vocabulary

Warm-Up

Jodi felt like skipping. The chain on her bicycle was finally fixed. Today was going to be fantastic!

Jodi and her dad were going on a bike ride. This bike ride was not like any other. It was to trace their steps back to where Jodi had found her first fossil.

It had been only a week since Jodi followed her dad up the bike path. The road twisted and turned. When Jodi became tired, they had stopped for lunch. "This seems like a mountain, not a hill," Jodi said.

Jodi's dad had laughed and said, "We both need to get in better shape."

Jodi smiled when she remembered what happened next. Just as she and her dad were about to continue on, the chain to her bike had broken. She huffed and puffed as they made their way back down the hill.

When they had stopped to rest again, Jodi saw something she would never forget. She found a flat rock with the print of a small animal on top. "What is this?" she asked her dad.

Jodi's dad had taken the fossil from her outstretched hand. Jodi smiled again as she remembered her dad's reply: "It is a story from the past."

Fill In the Blank
On a sheet of paper, use each of the vocabulary words in a sentence. Draw a blank line in place of each vocabulary word. Give your paper to another student. Have your partner fill in each blank with the correct vocabulary word.

Concept Vocabulary

The concept word for this lesson is **discovery.** A *discovery* is "something that is seen or found out for the first time." Jodi found out about fossils. She made a fossil discovery. Have you ever made a discovery? What did you discover?

Genre

Nonfiction is based on facts. It is about real people, things, or events.

Comprehension Skill

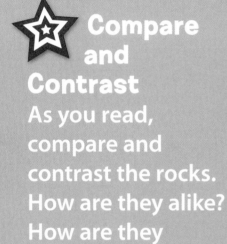

Compare and Contrast As you read, compare and contrast the rocks. How are they alike? How are they different?

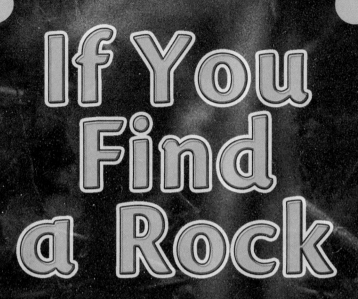

If You Find a Rock

by Peggy Christian

Photographs by
Barbara Hirsch Lember

Focus Questions

Why might someone collect rocks? Have you ever found a rock that reminds you of a certain person, place, or event?

If you find a rock,
a nice flat, rounded rock
that sits just right
in the crook of your finger,
then you have
a skipping rock.
You toss it out
in the water just so
and see it trip
across the surface,
making a chain
of spreading rings.

Maybe you find
a soft white rock—
a rock that feels dusty
in your fingers.
Then you have
a chalk rock,
and you use it
to make pictures
on the pavement.

Or you might find
a big mossy rock
by the side of
a long, steep trail.
Then you have
a resting rock,
and as you sit down
you feel
the cool moss
squush beneath you.

Then again,
you might find a rock
with a stripe running
all the way round it.
Trace the line
with your finger—
it must circle all the way.
You have
a wishing rock,
and you whisper
what you want
before you throw it.

If you find a rock—
a big rock—
by the edge of the water,
then you have found
a splashing rock.
When it hits the surface,
the water jumps
out of the way,
raining back down
on your outstretched hands.
The bigger the rock,
the wetter you get.

Maybe you find
a pile of small,
rounded pebbles.
Then you have found
sifting rocks,
and you can scoop up
a handful
and let them slide
slowly through
your fingers.

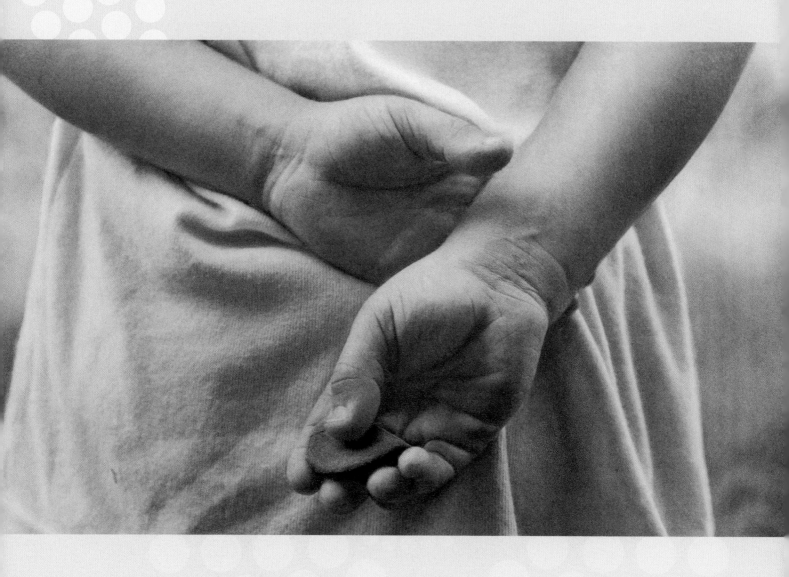

Or you might find a rock
whose water-smoothed surface
catches your eye.
If it feels easy
in your hand
when you rub it,
then you have found
a worry rock.
You rub it between
your fingers
and your troubles
are smoothed away.

Then again,
you might find a rock
sitting in a grassy field.
Push it over.
You have found
a hiding rock, and
in the cool, dark
underside live
all kinds of things
that creep and crawl and hide
out of sight.

If you find a rock—
a great rock—
that towers over you,
then you have found
a climbing rock.
Hold on with your toes and fingers,
grip hard as you
stretch up and pull
until you reach the top,
where you feel
much grander than you did
on the ground.

Maybe you will find
a twisting line of rocks
sticking up out of a creek.
Then you have found
crossing rocks,
which wait
to meet your feet
as you pass over
the water rushing away
all around you.

Or you might find
a rock with a print
of something else—
a leaf or a shell.
Then you have found
a fossil rock,
and you feel
the shape of something
that lived long, long ago
when the rock was young.

Then again,
you could find
a small, rounded rock
right in front
of your toe
as you go down
the sidewalk.
You have found
a walking rock,
and you kick it
ahead of you
and let it
lead you home.

If you find a rock—
a rock that's not
a skipping rock,
or a chalk rock,
or a resting rock,
or a wishing rock—
that's not
a splashing rock,
or a sifting rock,
or a worry rock,
or a hiding rock—
that's not even
a climbing rock,
or a crossing rock,
or a fossil rock,
or a walking rock,

but you like it anyway,
because it reminds you
of a place,
or a feeling,
or someone important—
then you have found
a memory rock,
and sometimes
those are the best
rocks of all.

Meet the Author

Peggy Christian

Christian grew up in the Rocky Mountains where she looked for rocks with her father, who was a geologist. Because of her parents, Christian grew to love the outdoors, which is reflected in her writing. She believes writers only do half the work when it comes to creating a book—readers make stories come alive by using their imaginations and exploring what the author has written.

Meet the Photographer

Barbara Hirsch Lember

Lember loved reading children's books with her daughters when they were young, so it was exciting for her to illustrate her own book, *A Book of Fruit.* Besides being a children's book illustrator, she is a professional photographer. Her photographs have won numerous awards and have been widely exhibited.

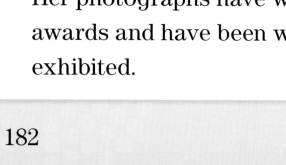

Theme Connections

Within the Selection

1. Where might you find a resting rock?
2. What kind of rock makes a good skipping rock?

Across Selections

3. How is "If You Find a Rock" like "Ants! They are hard workers!"?
4. How are the two stories different?

Beyond the Selection

5. What kinds of rocks do you like to collect?
6. Think about how "If You Find a Rock" adds to what you know about the theme Let's Explore.

Write about It!

Describe the most beautiful rock you have ever found.

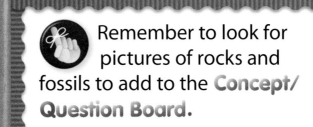

Remember to look for pictures of rocks and fossils to add to the **Concept/ Question Board.**

Science Inquiry

A STORY FROM THE PAST

When I was ten years old, my dad and I went rock hunting. Dad took me to an old creek bed.

There were so many rocks to choose from. We loaded rocks of every size and shape into the car. I wanted rocks for my rock collection. My dad wanted rocks to put around the trees in our backyard. When our car was full, we headed home.

I could not wait to see our rocks up close. Dad unloaded a flat rock. I bent over to look at it, and what I saw shocked me. It looked like the skeleton of a small animal.

"What is this?" I asked my dad.

"It is a fossil," he answered. "That rock has an imprint of an animal skeleton from long ago."

Today my job is to study rocks and fossils. I try to learn about Earth's history. I learn a lot about plants and animals of long ago from the rocks I find today.

184

1. What are some words in this story that let you know you are reading a narrative?

2. What might someone learn about the past from looking at a fossil?

3. Other than an imprint of a skeleton, what else might be on a fossil?

Try It!

As you work on your investigation, present some of your facts in the form of a narrative story to make the information more interesting.

Genre
Expository Text is written to inform or explain. It contains facts about real people, things, or events.

Comprehension Strategy

⭐ **Visualizing**
As you read, picture in your mind what is happening in the story.

HUNGRY HOPPERS
GRASSHOPPERS IN YOUR BACKYARD

by Nancy Loewen
illustrated by Brandon Reibeling

Focus Questions
Have you ever seen a grasshopper jumping in the grass? What other insects might you find in the grass?

Read the article to find the meanings of these words, which are also in "Hungry Hoppers":

- ✦ fussy
- ✦ dull
- ✦ sensing
- ✦ antennae
- ✦ cycle

Vocabulary Strategy

A definition is sometimes provided in the text right next to or near the word it is defining. Use **apposition** to find the meanings of *fussy* and *dull*.

Vocabulary

Warm-Up

Of the seasons winter, spring, summer, and fall, I do not know which season I like best. Some people think I am fussy, or hard to please, but that is only at the end of a season. By then, I am ready for the next season to begin.

In winter I cannot wait for it to snow. I like to build snow forts. By the end of winter, I am tired of the dull, or not bright, days.

Finally spring comes. I like sensing the green grass and flowers before they grow. I love the tulips and daffodils. By the end of spring I am ready to go swimming.

Then summer comes. There is so much to do that I do not know what to do first. One day last year I watched a grasshopper for the longest time. It was funny to see its antennae move back and forth. I like the still, quiet summer nights and the twinkling summer stars. But by the end of summer, I am tired of the heat.

That is when autumn arrives. I am ready for the crisp, cool days. I love pumpkins, rides in hay wagons, and frosty mornings.

I cannot figure out which season I like best. I guess I just like the cycle of the seasons!

GAME

Sentence Building
Work with a partner to create sentences using the vocabulary words. Choose a word from the list, and challenge your partner to make up a sentence using the word. Then switch roles. Continue until all the vocabulary words have been used.

Concept Vocabulary

The concept word for this lesson is **nature.** *Nature* is "everything in the world not made by people." Nature includes things such as plants, animals, and insects. What kinds of things from nature can you find outside?

HUNGRY HOPPERS

GRASSHOPPERS IN YOUR BACKYARD

by Nancy Loewen

illustrated by Brandon Reibeling

Focus Questions

Have you ever seen a grasshopper jumping in the grass? What other insects might you find in the grass?

BIG JUMPERS

Zip! Zing! What is that jumping in the grass?

Whiz! Whir! Grasshoppers! Look at how far they can jump!

If we're very still, maybe we can see a grasshopper close up.

There's one. Look at its back legs. Do you see how big they are? No wonder grasshoppers are such good jumpers!

A grasshopper can jump up to 20 times the length of its body. That's like a person being able to jump over four telephone poles placed end to end!

193

SENSING DANGER

Grasshoppers have big eyes, too. They let the grasshopper see things coming up behind it. Those thin stems near the grasshopper's eyes are called antennae. Grasshoppers use those to touch and smell.

A grasshopper always watches out for hungry creatures such as birds, frogs, and lizards. Its senses let it know when an enemy is near so it can quickly hop away.

This grasshopper is called a short-horned grasshopper because of the size of its antennae.

WHAT DO GRASSHOPPERS EAT?

Grasshoppers eat plants of all kinds. Most grasshoppers aren't too fussy. Anything green will do.

Do you see the little twig-like pieces on the grasshopper's mouth? Those are called palpi. The grasshopper uses them to taste food.

Farmers don't like having too many grasshoppers around. The hungry bugs can hurt crops growing in the fields.

TRICKY WINGS

There's a grasshopper flying away. Can you see its bright wings? Those colorful wings are usually hidden by another pair of dull, outer wings.

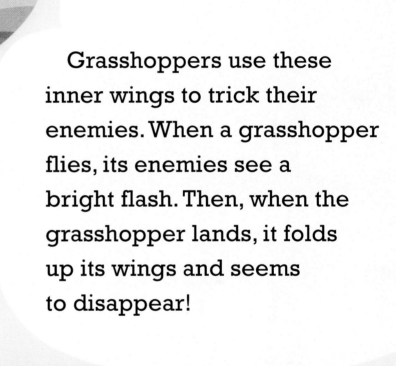

Grasshoppers use these inner wings to trick their enemies. When a grasshopper flies, its enemies see a bright flash. Then, when the grasshopper lands, it folds up its wings and seems to disappear!

A grasshopper's outer wings are tough like leather. They protect the inner wings, which unfold like fans when a grasshopper flies.

LIFE CYCLE OF A GRASSHOPPER

Shhh. Do you hear that buzzing sound? That's probably a male grasshopper trying to attract a mate. Males make this sound by rubbing their back legs against their wings.

About two weeks after mating, a female grasshopper lays 25 to 150 eggs in the soil. Her body makes a sticky glue that mixes with the soil. When the soil dries, it creates a case that protects the eggs.

A grasshopper's greatest enemy is fly larvae. Fly larvae are little worms that will turn into flies. They often feed on grasshopper eggs.

The grasshoppers die in late autumn, but the eggs live through winter. They hatch in the spring when the ground warms up.

The young grasshoppers look a lot like the adult grasshoppers. They're just smaller, and they don't have wings. Young grasshoppers are called nymphs.

The grasshopper nymph eats and eats all summer. As it grows, its shell gets too small and cracks off. This is called molting. A new, bigger covering is underneath the old covering. A nymph molts five or six times before becoming an adult.

When nymphs first hatch, they are almost white. After a few hours, their color and markings appear.

GRASSHOPPER GAMES

You might not notice grasshoppers much in the spring and early summer. That is when they are small and good at hiding. In late summer and into autumn, the grasshoppers are fully grown. It might seem as if they are everywhere.

Zip! Zing! Go ahead. See if you can catch one!

Meet the Author

Nancy Loewen

Loewen has written more than sixty books about many different topics, including insects, money, and natural disasters. She has won awards for her books from the American Library Association, the New York Public Library, and Parents' Choice.

Meet the Illustrator

Brandon Reibeling

Reibeling has illustrated more than twenty books. His illustrations are bright and colorful, like cartoons. Some of his books are funny, such as *Galactic Giggles*, *Animal Quack-Ups*, and *Chewy Chuckles*. His other books are more serious, such as *Kids Talk about Courage*.

Let's Explore

Theme Connections

Within the Selection

1. How far can a grasshopper jump?

2. What do grasshoppers eat?

Across Selections

3. How are grasshoppers and ants alike? How are they different?

Beyond the Selection

4. Have you ever seen a grasshopper jump? How far did it jump?

5. What are some other insects that can jump?

Write about It!

Describe a bug or insect you might see in your backyard.

 Remember to add pictures of grasshoppers and other insects to the Concept/ Question Board.

Science Inquiry

From Tadpole to Frog

Frogs lay their eggs in the water. After twenty-one days, a tadpole comes from the egg. A tadpole is a baby frog. It looks like a fish with a long tail. It breathes through gills. It eats small plants in the water called algae.

When a tadpole is five weeks old it begins to change. First it begins to grow hind legs. Then it begins to grow front legs. A tadpole begins to get lungs at this age too. Over time the tadpole looks more and more like a frog. Its tail becomes much smaller, and its legs continue to grow.

Eleven weeks after the female lays her eggs, the tadpole becomes a frog. It lives on land and in the water and eats insects and worms. If the new frog is a female, she will lay her own eggs early the next spring, and the cycle will begin again.

Think Link

1. Look at the diagram. Describe the third stage of a frog's life cycle.

2. How do you think the life cycle of a dog is different from the life cycle of a frog?

3. What happens eleven weeks after the female frog lays her eggs?

Try It!

As you work on your investigation, think about how you can use diagrams to show your facts.

211

Read the article to find the meanings of these words, which are also in "Birdhouse for Rent":

✦ rent
✦ vacant
✦ tenants
✦ deserted
✦ examined

Vocabulary Strategy

Word Structure, such as prefixes and suffixes, can help you determine the meanings of words. Determine the meanings of *deserted* and *examined.*

Vocabulary

Warm-Up

Birds are lucky creatures. They never have to pay rent. They just have to find a vacant nest or wait for the tenants to move out of one.

Some birds like living in nests that other birds have deserted. Other birds like living in brand-new nests. Maybe these birds examined old nests and decided they were just too messy. Perhaps they knew they would not be completely happy in a home that was not perfect.

Some people are that way too. They search and search for the right place to live. They look at house after house. Sometimes the houses are too small. Sometimes they are too big.

Like birds, people often choose to build homes. Some people need help building a home, but birds do not need help. Birds build their own homes.

Birds build nests in all shapes, sizes, and locations. Some nests are small, and others are big. Some birds build their nests in trees. Others build their nests on the ground. A bird works hard to build the perfect home.

Finally the nest is complete, and it is filled with baby birds. Even the baby birds do not have to pay rent!

GAME

Memory Game
Write each vocabulary word on an index card. Then write each word's meaning on its own card. Turn over and spread out the cards. Take turns with a partner matching each word with its meaning.

Concept Vocabulary

The concept word for this lesson is **habitat.** A *habitat* is "the place where an animal or plant naturally lives and grows." Polar bears live in the arctic. Black bears live in the forest. Why do you think animals needs to live in a certain type of habitat?

Birdhouse for Rent

by **Harriet Ziefert**

illustrated by Donald Dreifuss

Focus Questions

Are birds the only creatures that might live in a birdhouse? What other animals might use a birdhouse for their home?

I am a birdhouse. I was put in the ground at the beginning of July. As you can see, I am vacant. I have no tenants.

All summer, lots of birds flew over my roof. Some even stopped to rest. I was sure the bluebird who landed on my perch would come in, but he did not. A starling poked his beak in my doorway, but he didn't step inside.

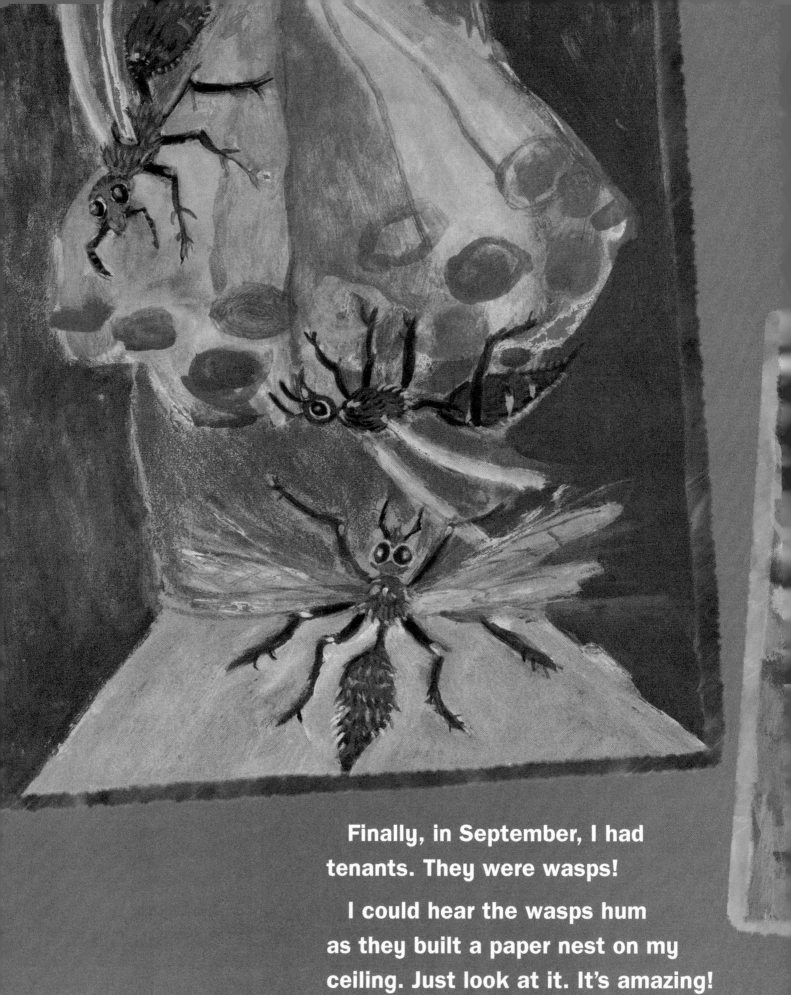

Finally, in September, I had
tenants. They were wasps!

I could hear the wasps hum
as they built a paper nest on my
ceiling. Just look at it. It's amazing!

In October, when the weather got cold, the wasps left. Chipmunks moved in. Oh, what messy tenants!

The chipmunks dragged in leaves, grass, sticks, and more acorns than I could count.

After a few weeks, I was ready for the chipmunks to leave, but they stayed all winter.

November was blowy. In December, it rained a lot.

January was icy. Heavy
snow fell in February.

Unfortunately, a
March storm snapped
my post.

Fortunately, the
chipmunks vacated.

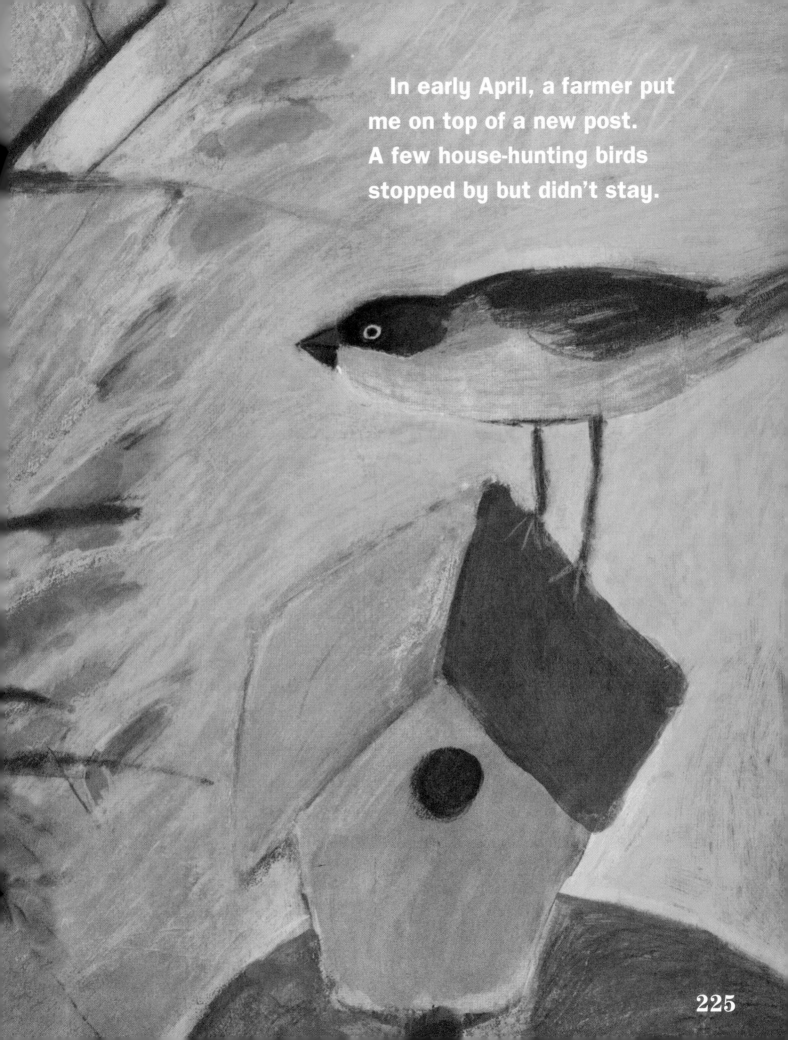

In early April, a farmer put
me on top of a new post.
A few house-hunting birds
stopped by but didn't stay.

One day a chickadee peeked into my doorway. He hopped all over my roof and examined me from all angles. He seemed to find everything to his liking.

He called to another bird, who was perched on a nearby branch. I thought, *That must be Mrs. Chickadee.* She came right over. She saw the place was snug and dry; the entrance was well above the floor, better for keeping out wind, rain, and enemies. She seemed pleased.

And so they moved in!

At first, Mr. and Mrs. Chickadee spent most of their days out of the house finding insects. But after a week or two, she stayed close to home and he did the food-collecting.

Mrs. Chickadee was building a nest!

After three days of hard work, Mrs. Chickadee nestled down. The next morning, I heard Mr. Chickadee calling softly.

Mrs. Chickadee gave him an eager welcome but did not get up. When she arched her back to reach for a nice, juicy caterpillar, I saw an egg!

230

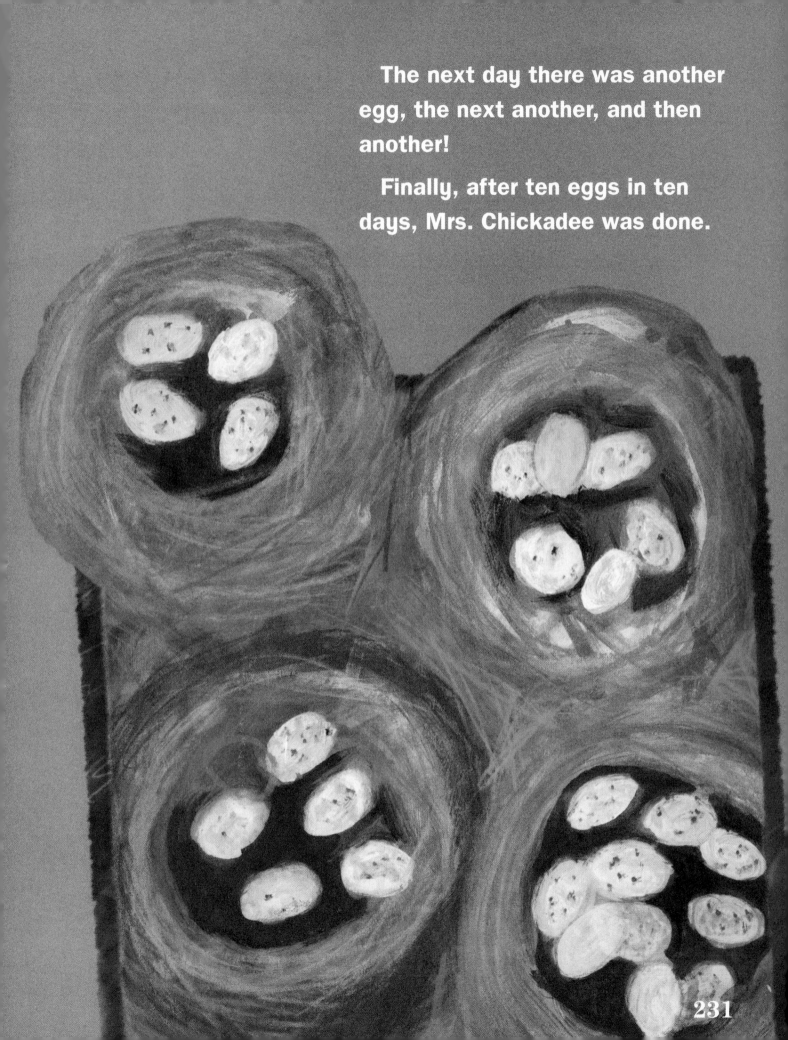

The next day there was another egg, the next another, and then another!

Finally, after ten eggs in ten days, Mrs. Chickadee was done.

For weeks, Mrs. Chickadee had been
spending nearly all of her time inside the
house. Now she stayed outside all day,
leaving her eggs deserted. But she did
cover them before she flew off, so an egg
thief wouldn't eat them.

Unfortunately, the farmer's cat was too smart for Mrs. Chickadee, and I watched him steal three of her eggs.

Finally, the eggs started to hatch. After two days, there were seven baby birds.

The babies always had their mouths wide open, begging to be fed. All together, I counted 600 feedings a day!

When the babies were
a few days old, the cat
returned, looking for more
to eat.

Mr. and Mrs. Chickadee
made a lot of noise and
chased him away. The
babies were safe!

As the babies grew, the place became quite crowded. I could hear little cheeps all day long, as if the babies were saying, *When can we go outside?*

And they did . . . in early June, when
they were big and plump and could fly!
They came in and out for a few days,
then they left my house completely.

I wonder who the next tenants will be.

275

Focus Questions What does "to live again a butterfly" mean? Have you ever seen a caterpillar turn into a butterfly?

Caterpillar

by Christina Rossetti *illustrated by Lori Lohstoeter*

Brown and furry
Caterpillar in a hurry,
Take your walk
To the shady leaf, or stalk,
Or what not,
Which may be the chosen spot.
No toad spy you,
Hovering bird of prey pass by you;
Spin and die,
To live again a butterfly.

Test-Taking Strategy: Identifying and Using Important Words

Pay attention to important words in directions and questions. These important words will help you find the correct answer.

Identifying and Using Important Words

Each question has important words. You need to listen to these words or read them carefully to answer the question correctly.

> **EXAMPLE**
> **Read this question to yourself. Think about the important words in the question.**
> **1. Which word means the SAME as *big*?**
>   ○ huge
>   ○ short
>   ○ light

The important words in the question are SAME and *big*. These words will help you know that the first answer is correct. *Huge* means the SAME as *big*.

A Different Look

"Are you ready?" Mr. Hall opened the door. "You two are going to see some very different things today."

Jen and Pablo walked outside. It looked the same as it always did.

"I do not see anything different, Dad," said Pablo.

"You will. Here is a good place to start." Mr. Hall pointed to the ground. "Look at that patch of green." He handed a magnifying glass to Jen.

"They look like tiny plants. What are they?" asked Jen.

"That is a kind of moss," said Mr. Hall. "Now look up there." He pointed to a tree in the yard.

"It looks like string hanging down from the tree," laughed Pablo.

"That is called Spanish moss. It is different from the moss on the ground." Mr. Hall pulled a small piece of moss from the tree. Pablo looked at it with the magnifying glass.

"Here is something else. Look at the yellow stuff on this plant." Mr. Hall showed Jen where to look.

"Yuck! That is awful, Dad!" Jen yelled. "What is it?"

Pablo grabbed the magnifying glass. "Jen is right. That is gross. What is it?"

"Tiny bugs. They are called aphids." Mr. Hall smiled at the two of them. "I told you that you would see some very different things today."

1. This story is probably a _____.
- ◯ fairy tale
- ◯ fantasy
- ◯ poem
- ◯ true story

2. Who is Mr. Hall?
- ◯ A neighbor
- ◯ The children's father
- ◯ A family friend
- ◯ The children's uncle

3. Pablo compares the Spanish moss to _____.
- ◯ string
- ◯ leaves
- ◯ wood
- ◯ bugs

4. What is the yellow stuff on the plant?
- ◯ Small flowers
- ◯ Dust
- ◯ Tiny bugs
- ◯ Honey

5. Which of these happens first in the story?
- ◯ Jen says, "Yuck!"
- ◯ Mr. Hall opens the door.
- ◯ Pablo looks at the bugs.
- ◯ They see a patch of green.

STOP

Around the Town

A community is made up of people and places. But not all communities are alike. Some are big, and others are small. Some have busy centers of town, and others have small, quiet corner stores. What is your community like?

Fine Art Theme Connection

Look at the painting *Chinatown, 2000* by Richard H. Fox.

- What do you see?
- Where do you think the people are going?
- How does this painting relate to the theme Around the Town?

BIG
Idea

What are some
places that might
be found in most
communities?

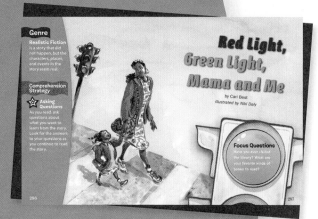

Read the article to find the meanings of these words, which are also in "Red Light, Green Light, Mama and Me":

- ✦ practice
- ✦ public
- ✦ recognize
- ✦ automatically
- ✦ perched

Vocabulary Strategy

Context Clues in the text help you find the meanings of words. Use context clues to find the meanings of *practice* and *public*.

Vocabulary

Warm-Up

Julie rounded third base and headed toward home. "We won! We won!" she screamed.

The crowd roared. It was the final game of the season, and the Tigers had ended up in first place. "Great job!" said Julie's mom.

"All your practice paid off," Julie's grandma said. "We should go out to dinner to celebrate."

"We will have to stop at home first," her mom said. "Julie needs to change her dusty clothes."

"I look fine," Julie protested.

"You can not go out in public like that. Someone will recognize you! We are not going to our usual pizza place. We are going to a new place."

Julie pulled off her baseball uniform. She automatically threw it into the dirty clothes pile.

Julie took a stamp out of her desk. She put a *W* on that day's game schedule. She was proud of the team's win.

Julie's mother was perched on the arm of the couch. "No more dust!" she smiled. "Now we can go eat a special dinner!"

Charades
Use the vocabulary words to play a game of charades with your classmates. Choose one of the words to act out. The first person to correctly identify the word and explain its meaning gets to take the next turn.

Concept Vocabulary

The concept word for this lesson is **community.** A *community* is "a place where people live, work, and play." Stores, houses, restaurants, and libraries are all part of a community. What makes your community special?

Genre

Realistic Fiction is a story that did not happen, but the characters, places, and events in the story seem real.

Comprehension Strategy

☆ Asking Questions

As you read, ask questions about what you want to learn from the story. Look for the answers to your questions as you continue to read the story.

Red Light, Green Light, Mama and Me

by Cari Best

illustrated by Niki Daly

Focus Questions

Have you ever visited the library? What are your favorite kinds of books to read?

"Red light, green light, one, two, three," I sing as Mama and I hurry across the morning street.

Around the corner. Past the mailbox.

Down the dusty steps.
I run like mad to keep up
with Mama's long legs.

"Here's where I get my blueberry muffin," she says. "Two muffins today, Lenny. Lizzie's coming to work with me." I like when Lenny says I look just like Mama.

I skip and jump instead of walk. Mama holds my hand tight.

Finally she says, "This is it, Lizzie girl. The Downtown Public Library." My mama must be the most important person in the whole city.

Inside Mama's library there is a Reading Room. It is so quiet that I can hear my shoes clicking across the floor. And there are millions of books. High, low, and in the middle, too. No wonder Mama is so smart. "Do you read all day?" I ask. "Not *all* day," she says. "You'll see."

Down the hall there are lots of mailboxes. Mama gets more mail than the President. "Toby, you're here bright and early," she says to someone who's already working. "Granny's caught the flu, so Lizzie's a working girl today."

"Hey, Lizzie!" says Toby. "How about we all meet for lunch? I have enough peanut butter and bananas for you, me, and all the pigeons in the city."

293

"Can I come, too?" asks a teeny weeny voice from behind a great big desk. It's Flo. I recognize her voice from talking to her on the telephone when I call Mama at work.

294

All of a sudden a man with a mustache and hair like a French poodle comes *skating* in! Mama says it's amazing Albert. "You must be Lizzie," he says. Mama says Albert knows everything.

"See you at lunchtime," we tell Albert on our way to the Children's Room.

I know Mama's desk as soon as I see the bumpy crocodile I made for her last year. I see puppets and puzzles and music and crayons. And a lot of the same books that Mama and I read together at home.

If I had Mama's job, I'd look at books all day, smell them, and take home all the ones with new covers.

But Mama is way too busy to read to me now. She talks and talks and talks on the telephone. When she is finished, she comes running over. "Lizzie, I'm going to tell 'The Three Little Pigs' at story time. Would you be the Big Bad Wolf?"

I'm not sure if I can huff and puff like Mama does when she's the Big Bad Wolf at home. But I say okay anyway. I practice hard in front of the mirror.

Soon every pillow has someone sitting on it. Mama looks beautiful in her tiger lily dress and is all ready to start, but I have a thousand butterflies. I listen for my part.

Then I HUFF and PUFF and *BLOW* the house down!

300

After the story Mama has a hug for everybody. And a big one just for me. "I think it's about time for the Big Bad Wolf to have lunch," she whispers.

"Working makes you *really* hungry," I say.

Out on the library steps, Toby, Flo, and
Albert are waiting to have a city picnic. Toby's
peanut butter lunch is good. The pigeons
love it! For dessert I help Albert buy sky blue
ices from Luigi.

After lunch, while Mama does her reading work, Flo asks me to stamp a big pile of papers with today's date. Then she stamps my hand. "Today is a very important day," she says.

In the middle of my stamping a little boy asks me which book he should choose. I show him where to find a really good one.

"This is the one *I* like best," I say.

Just then I see Albert waving to me. "Lizzie, help!" he calls in a loud whisper. Lizzie, Lizzie, Lizzie. *Everyone* needs me! "This lady wants to know why pigeons don't fall off the library roof when they sleep," says Albert. Albert and I search a long time for the answer. Finally we find it!

"'When a bird sleeps, its toes automatically lock around wherever it's perched. And they don't open until the bird wants them to.'"

"Like this," says Albert, closing and opening his hands.

I can't wait to tell Mama all about how pigeons sleep. But first I have something very important to do.

I draw a little.
Write a little.
And cut out a lot.

When I am finished, I have a city of bookmarks: one for Toby, one for Flo, one for Albert, and one for Mama. And one for me.

It's almost time for the Downtown Library to close. I help Mama put back the puzzle pieces, the puppets, and the chairs. Mama sticks her new bookmark inside a big fat book on her desk. Right next to the bumpy crocodile.

Downstairs, Toby, Flo, and Albert are getting ready to go home, too. When I give them their skyscraper bookmarks, they give me a giant work family *squeeze!*

Then Mama and I and all the other work families in the city say good-bye to the tall buildings, the Lennys and the Luigis, and the pigeons that sleep on the library roof without falling off.

Red light, green light, Mama and me.

Meet the Author

Cari Best

Best uses her childhood memories to come up with ideas for her writing. Her story *Three Cheers for Catherine the Great!* is about her Russian grandmother. Best is a former children's librarian and likes to watch butterflies and birds, work in her garden, take bike rides, and walk her dog.

Meet the Illustrator

Niki Daly

Daly was born and raised in Cape Town, South Africa. He started drawing when he was a little boy using pencil stubs handed down to him from his uncle. He moved and lived in London for a while, but he returned to South Africa to be close to his family. He loves to see children use their imaginations to change ordinary things into something fun and exciting.

Theme Connections

Within the Selection

1. Where does Lizzie's mama work?

2. Why does Lizzie think her mama must be the most important person in the city?

Beyond the Selection

3. In "Red Light, Green Light, Mama and Me," Lizzie's mom is a librarian. What job do you want to have when you grow up?

4. Think about how "Red Light, Green Light, Mama and Me" adds to what you know about communities.

Write about It!

Make a list of all the things you think a librarian does. Compare your list with others.

Remember to look for pictures of libraries and other places around your town to add to the Concept/Question Board.

Saturdays, Mom, and Me

On Saturdays I like to sleep in late. I snuggle under the blankets until I am ready to get up. Then I go downstairs and eat a bowl of cereal.

After I eat breakfast, I get dressed. If I have soccer practice, Mom drives me there. She picks me up too. If I do not have soccer practice, I just play in my room.

I guess I am pretty lazy on Saturdays, but my mom is not. She gets up early and makes a grocery list. She goes to the store while I play soccer. Then she does laundry or works on the computer.

Mom says Saturday is her "catch-up" day at home. She works at the library all week. Mom says she loves her job. Someday I want to be a librarian too.

Then I will not have lazy Saturdays anymore. I will have to work hard like Mom.

1. What word in the first sentence lets you know this story is a narrative?

2. Explain why some parents have to get up early on Saturdays.

3. How are Saturdays different for the narrator and his mom?

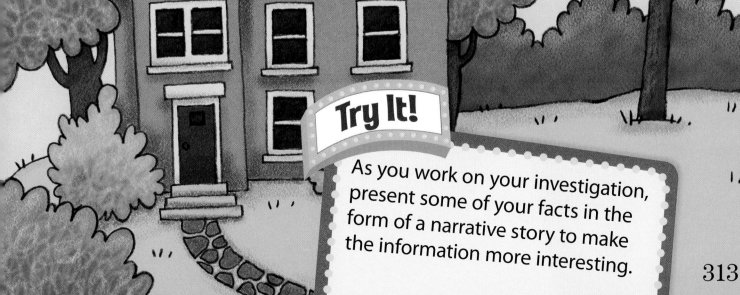

Try It!

As you work on your investigation, present some of your facts in the form of a narrative story to make the information more interesting.

In The Money: A Book About Banking

by Nancy Loewen
illustrated by Brad Fitzpatrick

Focus Questions
Why do people keep money at the bank? Do you keep money at a bank?

316   317

Read the article to find the meanings of these words, which are also in "In the Money: A Book About Banking":

✦ vault
✦ withdrawals
✦ borrow
✦ employees
✦ deposits

Vocabulary Strategy

The vocabulary words *withdrawals*, *employees*, and *deposits* are plural. Use **word structure** to determine the meaning of each of these words.

Vocabulary

Warm-Up

"Let's go put your birthday money in the bank," Ina's mom said. "They will safely store it for you in the vault."

"But I want to spend it," Ina said.

"You can still spend your money. We can come to the bank and make withdrawals," said Ina's mom. But she also told Ina how smart it is to save money. "Then you might not have to borrow it in the future," she said.

In the bank lobby, Ina was amazed. People were everywhere. Some people were bank employees. They were sorting through stacks of money.

314

Other people were there to make deposits, just like Ina.

Ina and her mom spoke to the bank employee. "What happens if a dollar bill gets torn?" Ina asked.

"That bill would be destroyed. A new one would be made to replace it," the woman said.

"I am glad I am putting my money in the bank," Ina said. "Now I can save it. It will be safe."

"Here is your receipt, Ina," the bank employee said. "Be sure to keep it so you have a record of your deposit. Thanks for coming in today!"

Memory Game
Write each vocabulary word on an index card. Then write each word's meaning on its own card. Turn over and spread out the cards. Take turns with a partner matching each word with its meaning.

Concept Vocabulary

The concept word for this lesson is **earn.** *Earn* means "to get money for the work you do." A teacher earns money by teaching children. A mail carrier earns money by delivering the mail. How do you want to earn money when you grow up?

Genre

Expository Text is written to inform or explain. It contains facts about real people, things, or events.

Comprehension Strategy

⭐ Clarifying
As you read, check to make sure you understand what you are reading and clarify any difficult words or phrases.

Focus Questions

Why do people keep money at the bank? Do you keep money at a bank?

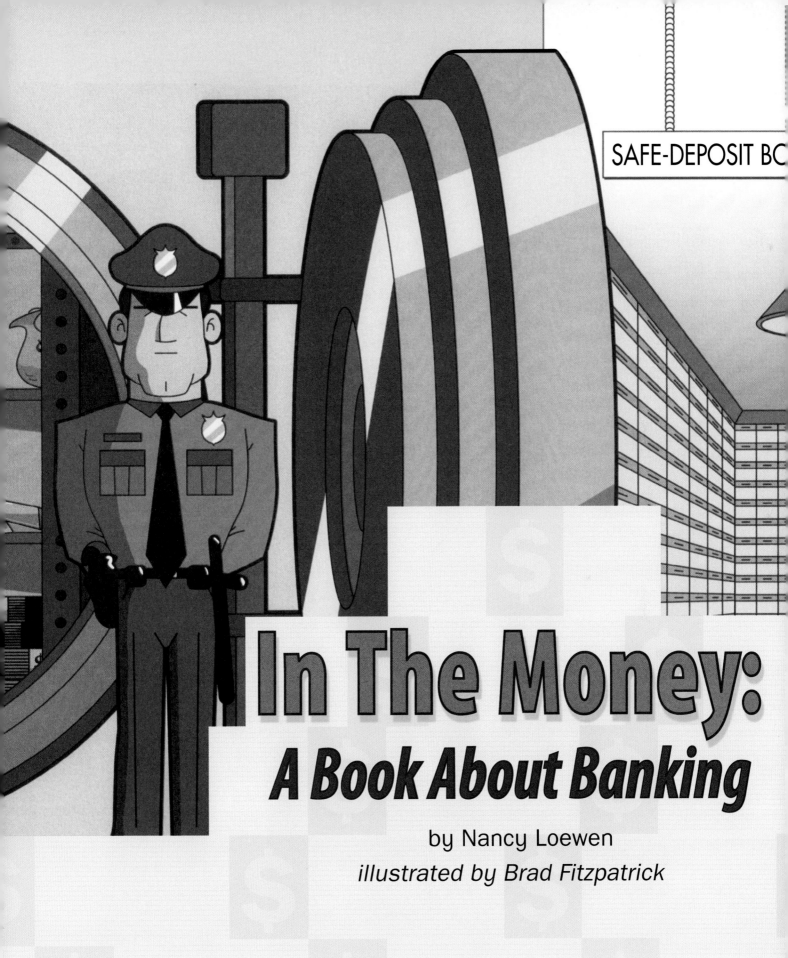

SAFE-DEPOSIT BO

In The Money:
A Book About Banking

by Nancy Loewen

illustrated by Brad Fitzpatrick

"Good morning! Time to get up!" Mom said.

"I don't have to go to school today," David said. "It's Take Your Child to Work Day. You're going to show me what you do as a loan officer at the bank."

"That's right," Mom replied. "There's a lot to see at the bank, so get moving!"

"How long have banks been around?
Did you have banks when you were a kid?"
David asked his mom.

"I'm not that old!" she said with a laugh. "Banks have been around for hundreds of years. The very first banks were in ancient Mesopotamia. People used grain as money. Temples and palaces offered people safe places to store it."

In 1781, the first official bank in the United States opened in Philadelphia, Pennsylvania.

When they got to the bank, Mom showed David around. The bank had just opened and a lot of people were working.

Banks come in all sizes. Some bank buildings cover an entire block. Others are small offices within grocery stores.

Employees were typing at computers or talking on the phone—sometimes both at the same time. Others were sorting through stacks of paper. In the lobby, a couple of people were loading cash into the automatic teller machine, or ATM.

"Do you want to watch the tellers?" Mom asked.

"What's a teller?" asked David. "Are they like story tellers?"

"Tellers are the people who help the customers," Mom answered.

"But sometimes we like to tell stories, too," a young woman said with a smile. "Hi, David, I'm Holly."

"Could you show David his savings account?" Mom asked Holly. "Here's his account number."

"No problem," said Holly. She typed the number into the computer.

Bank accounts of all kinds are identified by a long number. No two account numbers are alike.

On the computer screen, David could see the deposits and withdrawals he had made. He also saw a small deposit that he didn't remember making.

"Where did that money come from?" he asked.

"That's the interest you earned on your account," Holly replied. "Interest is what the bank pays people to keep their money here."

"When people borrow money, they pay interest to the bank," Mom added. "Those are the two main jobs of a bank: to be a safe place for people to keep their money, and to lend money to people for big purchases."

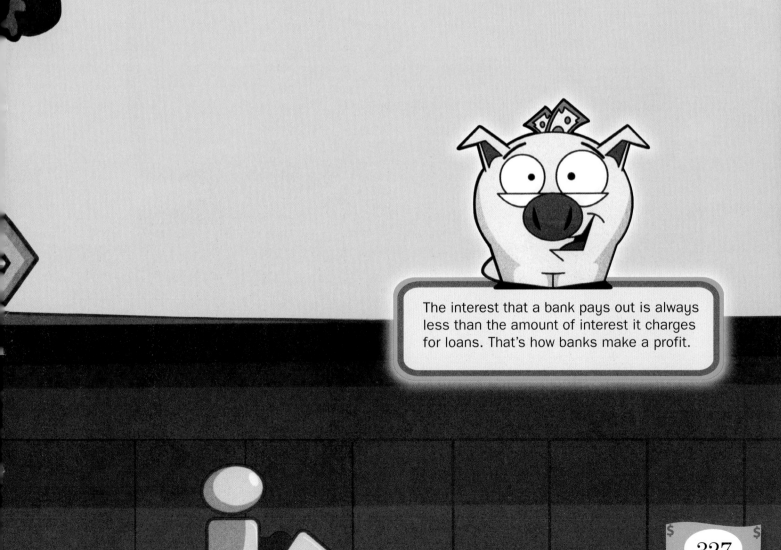

The interest that a bank pays out is always less than the amount of interest it charges for loans. That's how banks make a profit.

David sat on a stool and watched as Holly took cash and checks from customers and put them into a drawer. For every transaction, she printed out a receipt and gave it to the customer. One man cashed a check for $200. Holly counted out $20 bills so fast, her fingers were a blur.

"Wow! You could be a magician!" David exclaimed.

A check is like a letter to the bank from another bank. It tells the bank to give money to whomever is named on the check.

A woman came in with a badly torn $10 bill. Holly took the bill and gave her a crisp new one.

"What happens to that old money?" David asked.

Federal Reserve Banks are located in these cities: Boston, New York, Philadelphia, Cleveland, Richmond, Atlanta, Chicago, St. Louis, Minneapolis, Kansas City, Dallas, and San Francisco.

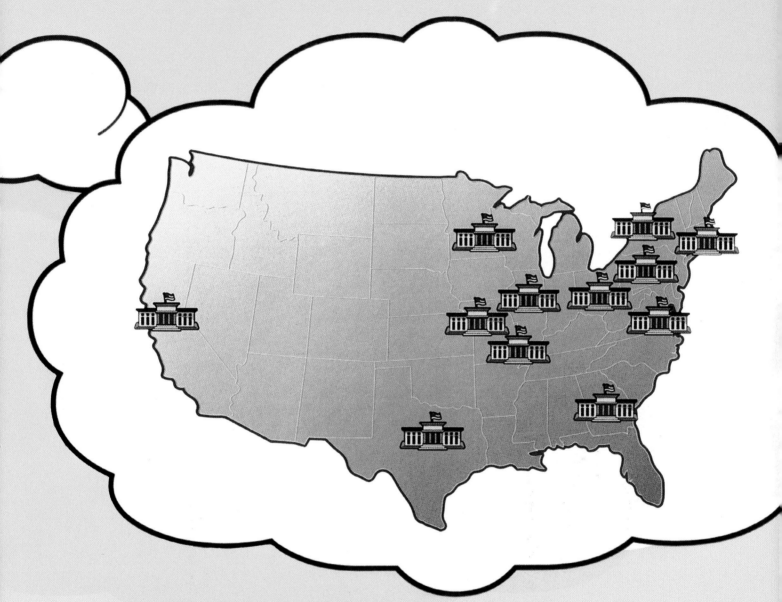

"The bank sends old bills to a special bank called the Federal Reserve Bank. The damaged bills and coins are destroyed, and we get new ones," Holly said. "There are 12 Federal Reserve Banks in the United States. Each one serves a different area. These banks are kind of like banks for banks. Even the government uses these banks."

Next, Mom showed David the bank's vault and the room with the safe-deposit boxes.

"The bank keeps its money in the vault," Mom said. "The vault is totally safe. It's even fireproof. See those boxes over there? Those are safe-deposit boxes. People rent the boxes to store valuable things like jewelry or legal papers," Mom told David.

SAFE-DEPOSIT BOX

A safe-deposit box is very private and secure. No one can open the box without the renter's permission.

333

Next, Mom had an appointment with a man who wanted to borrow money to buy a new car. David watched while his mom looked over the loan application papers and asked a few questions.

"Everything looks good," she said. "You should be getting your loan in a few days."

"Great!" he said.

After the man left, David asked, "Why do people need loans?"

"Well, most people don't have enough money to buy expensive things like cars and houses," his mom said. "Sometimes people need money to send their kids to college or to start a business."

Before making loans, banks look over a person's financial history. This includes how much money the person earns, how much debt the person has, how much the person owns, and if the person pays bills on time.

"I bet I know what you like the most about your job," David said.

"What?" Mom asked.

"Seeing how happy people are when you tell them they're going to get the money they need," David said.

"You're right," Mom said with a grin.

Meet the Author

Nancy Loewen

Loewen has written more than sixty books about many different topics, including insects, money, and natural disasters. She has won awards for her books from the American Library Association, the New York Public Library, and Parents' Choice.

Meet the Illustrator

Brad Fitzpatrick

Fitzpatrick has illustrated books written in both English and Spanish. He uses bold lines and bright colors to make drawings that may remind you of cartoons. He illustrated the "Money Matters" series, a group of books about banking. These books help readers learn about taxes, trading, and the history of money. His illustrations really help readers understand this information, and they make it fun to learn all about money!

Theme Connections

Within the Selection

1. What did the very first banks use as money?

2. Where did these banks store their "money"?

Across Selections

3. In "Red Light, Green Light, Mama and Me" and "In the Money: A Book About Banking," how do Lizzie and David learn about their parents' jobs?

Beyond the Selection

4. Why might a community have more than one bank?

Write about It!

Describe what you would buy if you saved fifty dollars.

Remember to look for newspaper articles about banks and other places in your community to add to the **Concept/Question Board.**

Choices

Earning Money

There are many different ways to earn money. People who live in the country might choose to be farmers. They can earn money by growing crops. Their crops can be sold at small markets or to large stores.

Some people choose to work in the city. They may drive a long or short way to get to their jobs. There are many ways to earn money in the city. Some people earn money by keeping us safe. Others work in office buildings or grocery stores.

Spending and Saving Money

It is important to be smart about spending and saving money. A person should not spend more money than he or she has saved. How to spend and save money is a choice people must make every day.

Think Link

1. How is the second heading helpful?

2. How might a farmer make money?

3. What are some choices people have about money?

Try It!

As you work on your investigation, think about how you could use headings to organize your information.

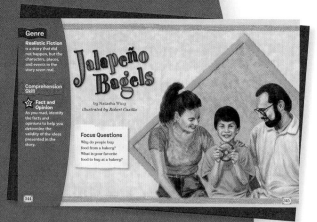

Jalapeño Bagels

by Natasha Wing
illustrated by Robert Casilla

Focus Questions

Why do people buy food from a bakery? What is your favorite food to buy at a bakery?

Read the article to find the meanings of these words, which are also in "Jalapeño Bagels":

✦ culture
✦ international
✦ ingredients
✦ dough
✦ jalapeño

Vocabulary Strategy

A definition is sometimes provided in the text right next to or near the word it is defining. Use **apposition** to find the meanings of *culture* and *jalapeño*.

Vocabulary

Warm-Up

Jose liked to spend time working in the garden with his grandfather. Jose's grandfather often spoke of his Mexican culture, or customs and beliefs. Jose loved to hear about his international travels too.

Jose plucked the peppers from the plants. He listened to his grandfather tell a story about France. "The best bread in the world is in France," said his grandfather. His grandfather talked about the ingredients in French bread. Jose could almost see the baker knead the dough. He could almost taste the delicious bread.

"Come on, you two!" Jose's grandmother called. "Come inside for lunch."

"Can we have French bread?" Jose asked his grandmother.

"How about tacos instead?" she replied.

Jose had his heart set on French bread. "I have an idea!" said Jose's grandfather. "Come with me, Jose!"

They drove to the bakery and came back with a loaf of French bread.

"Was it as good as you dreamed?" asked his grandmother.

"All it needed was a jalapeño, or small hot pepper!" laughed Jose.

Flash Cards
Make a set of flash cards with the vocabulary words. Write the word on one side and its definition on the other side. Use the flash cards to review the vocabulary words and definitions. Then ask a partner to use the cards to quiz you.

Concept Vocabulary

The concept word for this lesson is **business**. A *business* is "a company or other organization that buys and sells goods, makes products, or provides services." A bakery is a type of business. Can you name other types of businesses?

Jalapeño Bagels

by Natasha Wing

illustrated by Robert Casilla

Focus Questions

Why do people buy food from a bakery? What is your favorite food to buy at a bakery?

"What should I bring to school on Monday for International Day?" I ask my mother. "My teacher told us to bring something from our culture."

"You can bring a treat from the *panaderia*," she suggests. Panaderia is what Mama calls our bakery. "Help us bake on Sunday—then you can pick out whatever you want."

"It's a deal," I tell her. I like helping at the bakery. It's warm there, and everything smells so good.

Early Sunday morning, when it is still dark, my mother wakes me up.

"Pablo, it's time to go to work," she says.

We walk down the street to the bakery. My father turns on the lights. My mother turns on the ovens. She gets out the pans and ingredients for *pan dulce*. Pan dulce is Mexican sweet bread.

I help my mother mix and knead the dough. She shapes rolls and loaves of bread and slides them into the oven. People tell her she makes the best pan dulce in town.

"Maybe I'll bring pan dulce to school," I tell her.

Next we make *empanadas de calabaza*—
pumpkin turnovers. I'm in charge of
spooning the pumpkin filling. Mama folds
the dough in half and presses the edges with
a fork. She bakes them until they are flaky
and golden brown. Some customers come to
our bakery just for her turnovers.

"Maybe I'll bring empanadas de calabaza
instead."

"You'll figure it out," she says. "Ready to make *chango* bars?" Chango means "monkey man."

Mama lets me pour in the chocolate chips and nuts. When she's not looking, I pour in more chocolate chips.

"I could bring chango bars. They're my favorite dessert."

"Mine, too," says Mama. "This batch should be especially good. I put in extra chips."

My father calls from the back room.
"Pablo! Come help me with the bagels!"
Papa speaks English and Yiddish. He
learned Yiddish from his family in New York
City. I know some words, too. *Bubbe* means
"grandmother." He uses my bubbe's recipe to
make the bagels.

First he makes the dough in a big metal bowl. Then he rolls it out into a long rope shape. He cuts off pieces and shows me how to connect the ends in a circle. We put the circles on trays where they sit and rise.

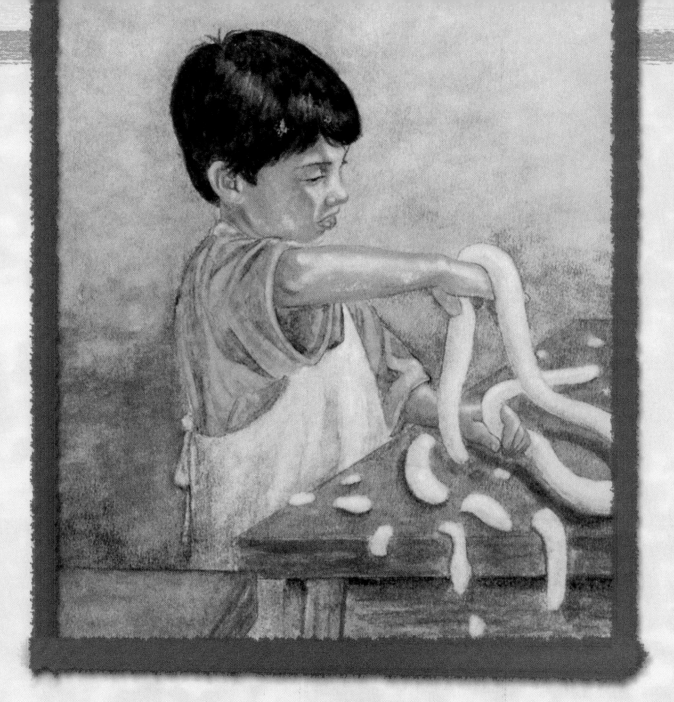

While we are waiting my father makes *challah,* Jewish braided bread. He lets me practice braiding challah dough at my own counter. It's a lot like braiding hair. The customers say it is almost too beautiful to eat.

"Maybe I'll bring a loaf of challah to school," I tell Papa. He smiles.

When the bagel dough has risen, he
boils the bagels in a huge pot of water and
fishes them out with a long slotted spoon. I
sprinkle on poppy seeds and sesame seeds,
and then they go in the oven.

"Maybe I could bring sesame-seed bagels
with cream cheese."

"No *lox?*" Lox is smoked salmon. My father's favorite bagel is pumpernickel with a smear of cream cheese and lox.

I crinkle my nose. "Lox tastes like fish. Jam is better."

My mother joins us and helps my father make another batch of bagels—*jalapeño* bagels. My parents use their own special recipe. While Papa kneads the dough, Mama chops the jalapeño *chiles*. She tosses them into the dough and adds dried red peppers. We roll, cut, make circles, and let them rise. I can't wait until they are done because I am getting hungry.

"Have you decided what you're going to bring to school?" asks Mama.

"It's hard to choose. Everything is so good," I tell her. I look at Papa. "Except for lox."

"You should decide before we open," warns Mama, "or else our customers will buy everything up."

I walk past all the sweet breads, chango bars, and bagels.

I think about my mother and my father and all the different things they make in the bakery.

And suddenly I know exactly what I'm going to bring.

"Jalapeño bagels," I tell my parents. "And I'll spread them with cream cheese and jam."

"Why jalapeño bagels?" asks Papa.

"Because they are a mixture of both of you. Just like me!"

Meet the Author

Natasha Wing

Wing became interested in writing children's books after reading one as an adult. She said, "When you put two things together, such as a story and illustrations, the result is greater than what you expected." *Jalapeño Bagels* is her second book for children.

Meet the Illustrator

Robert Casilla

Casilla began illustrating after graduating from the School of Visual Arts. He said, "I find great rewards and satisfaction in illustrating for children." He enjoys working with watercolors for his illustrations.

Theme Connections

Within the Selection

1. Why does Pablo like helping at his parents' bakery?

2. What food does Pablo decide to take to school for International Day?

Across Selections

3. How do Lizzie from "Red Light, Green Light, Mama and Me" and Pablo help their parents?

Beyond the Selection

4. Have you ever followed a recipe? What did you make?

Write about It!

Pretend you own a bakery. Write about the foods you sell.

Remember to add items about your community to the **Concept/Question Board.**

Family Tradition

Each year on my birthday my grandma makes chopped tortilla salad. It is a family recipe. My great-great-grandmother created it years ago. Now my grandma makes it for me. Grandma says the recipe has changed a little over the years. Each cook has made a small change. I would not change anything though. It is my favorite meal!

Making the Salad

Combine lettuce, jalapeños, olives, tomato, and onion in a large bowl. Mix these together. Next add the tortillas.

In another bowl, combine taco sauce, lime juice, and olive oil. Stir this well.

Pour the salad dressing over the lettuce mixture, and stir.

To finish, my grandma always puts one sliced jalapeño on top. This helps the salad look nice.

Enjoy!

Genre

How-To Text tells people how to do something.

Feature

Headings tell what a paragraph is going to be about.

Chopped Tortilla Salad

INGREDIENTS FOR Chopped Tortilla Salad	INGREDIENTS FOR the Salad Dressing
2 heads of romaine lettuce	2 T. taco sauce
3 T. sliced jalapeños	1 lime, juiced
3 T. salad olives	1/4 c. olive oil
1 tomato, chopped	
1/2 red onion, chopped	
1 c. broken tortillas	

Think Link

1. How is the heading in this story helpful?

2. Who was the first person in the family to make chopped tortilla salad?

3. What is the last step in making the salad?

Try It!

As you work on your investigation, remember to use headings to organize your information.

361

Read the article to find the meanings of these words, which are also in "Out and About at City Hall":

- ✦ council
- ✦ mayor
- ✦ elect
- ✦ cashier
- ✦ taxes
- ✦ routes

Vocabulary Strategy

Context Clues in the text help you find the meanings of words. Use context clues to find the meanings of *elect* and *routes*.

Vocabulary

Warm-Up

My dad is running for city council. He wants to work with the mayor to keep our city safe.

Dad has to be elected before he can be on city council. I would vote for my dad, but I am not old enough to vote. I am going to tell everyone about my dad. Maybe they will elect him.

Dad knows our city. He has had many different jobs. When I was born, he was a cashier in a store. No matter where we go, Dad always meets someone who knew him then. "Your store had the best events," they always say.

That makes Dad smile. "I always hated to charge a fee for anything,"

he says. "But that is how stores make money." Dad says things did not cost as much then. He says taxes were lower too.

When I was three years old, Dad changed jobs. "He was a transportation expert," Mom says. Dad drove a city bus. Then he *really* got to know the city! He drove more routes than any other bus driver.

My dad wants to make sure everyone in our city has everything they need.

I am going to make a banner to help my dad get elected. It is going to say: Vote for my dad—he knows our city!

GAME

Guessing Game
Choose a partner. Ask your partner, "What word means 'a person in charge of paying or receiving money'?" After correctly guessing *cashier,* it is your partner's turn to choose a word for you to guess. Review all the vocabulary words.

Concept Vocabulary

The concept word for this lesson is **election.** An *election* is "the act of choosing by vote." An election can decide who will be mayor. An election can decide how much money schools will receive. Have you ever had a class election? Whom or what did you vote for?

Genre

Expository Text is written to inform or explain. It contains facts about real people, things, or events.

Comprehension Skill

⭐ **Drawing Conclusions**

As you read, use the information in the text to draw conclusions about the characters or the events in the story.

Focus Questions

Who works at city hall? Why is city hall an important part of a community?

OUT AND ABOUT AT
CITY HALL

by Nancy Garhan Attebury

illustrated by Zachary Trover

Good morning! My name is Penny, and I'm the Rushford city manager. I work here at city hall.

What do you think makes a city a good place to live? Parks? A lot of stores and restaurants? Those things are important, but a city also needs good roads, police and fire protection, and much more.

A city manager oversees many city workers. Four years of college are needed for the job. He or she needs to be very organized and willing to be a leader.

My job as the city manager is to make sure people in Rushford have all the basic things they need. Clean water, sewer service, and garbage pick-up are just some of those needs.

I also schedule fun public activities, such as parades and picnics. On the wall is a picture from last year's Fourth of July celebration.

The city is responsible for the disposal of its citizens' sewage. Sewer pipes run from each building to larger pipes beneath city streets. These larger pipes carry sewage to a wastewater treatment plant, where the water is cleaned and disinfected.

The City of Rushford

Services	Who Provides Them
Water and Sewer	Water Department
Garbage	Sanitation Department, Recycling Center
Streets and Roads	Road Department
Fire Protection	Fire Department
Health Care	Public Health Nurse and Staff
Law Enforcement	Police Department
Transportation	Department of Transportation

This chart shows some of the services Rushford provides. Bigger cities may offer more services, and smaller cities may offer less. Some cities, for example, have a parks and recreation department. That department takes care of the city parks, ice rinks, swimming pools, and athletic fields.

City records are saved on computers. Some records show things such as who paid their water bill or who owns a piece of land. Other records show how much city workers are paid or where underground sewer pipes lie.

People who own homes and businesses in the city pay taxes for city services. These services include police and fire protection, road care, public transportation, libraries, and animal control.

372

Other city services, such as water and sewer, are called public utilities. Each month, citizens receive a public utility bill from the city. They can mail their payment, drop it off at the cashier window, or pay online.

In some cities, private companies provide utilities. In these cities, citizens can choose which company they want.

Have you ever ridden on a city bus? At city hall we have maps of bus routes. The bus system is one of many kinds of public transportation. Anybody may use it, but there is a fee to ride.

Kids your age can buy a student pass that is good for many rides, or you can pay each time you ride. You could ride to the library or swimming pool on a city bus. Light rail systems (also called streetcars or city trains) and subways are two other kinds of public transportation.

A bus schedule shows the time a bus arrives at a bus stop. It also shows what time it leaves the stop. A bus map shows different routes. The routes are shown in different colors. Most city buses cover the same routes every day.

The city council meets in this big room. Adult citizens vote to elect the council members. Each council member represents, or speaks for, a different part of the city and the citizens who live there.

Ideas for City Funding:

Library improvements	$140,000
New science museum	$257,000
New parking meters	$10,000
Bike trail	$13,750

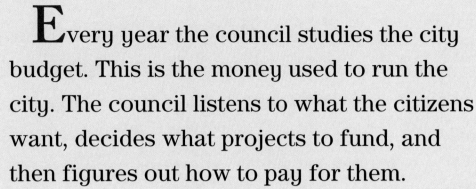

Every year the council studies the city budget. This is the money used to run the city. The council listens to what the citizens want, decides what projects to fund, and then figures out how to pay for them.

In addition to paying taxes directly to the city, people pay an extra tax when they put gas in their cars. Those tax dollars go to the state government first, then some of the money is given back to the cities. That money goes into a general fund to help pay for services managed from city hall.

This is Gary, our city recorder. He keeps a written record of what happens in city council meetings. These notes are called minutes.

For example, the city council may vote on where to put a new park. Gary writes down what the council members said and how they voted.

A city also makes money from a variety of fees. Money collected from parking meters, fines, and the sale of permits and licenses are added to the city budget.

Right next to Gary is the mayor's office. Mayor Perez works at city hall, too. She leads our city government. The city government decides how the city will do things.

The city government works with county and state governments to make sure city projects are safe for people and the environment. Mayor Perez attends many public events. She talks to as many people as she can so she has a better understanding of the citizens she represents.

Adults in a city vote to elect the mayor. Several people may want the job. Voters choose a mayor who thinks like them and can do what they want. A mayor supports projects that will make the city a good place to live.

It's important to know how your city works. It's also important for you to let us know how we can make Rushford an even better place for everyone. Thanks for visiting city hall today!

Meet the Author

Nancy Garhan Attebury

Attebury has written several nonfiction books and magazine articles for children. She not only writes for children but also works with other authors to help them improve their own writing. Other books she has written in the Field Trips series are about going to the bank, the hospital, and the U.S. mint.

Meet the Illustrator

Zachary Trover

Trover has illustrated many of the books in the Field Trips series, including books about visiting the dentist, the theater, the newspaper, and the baseball stadium. One of his books, *Guatemala ABCs*, teaches readers all about Guatemala and helps them learn new words too.

Theme Connections

Within the Selection

1. What is the job of a city manager?

2. What are two kinds of public transportation mentioned in the story?

Across Selections

3. How is "Out and About at City Hall" like "In the Money: A Book About Banking"?

4. How are the stories different?

Beyond the Selection

5. Who do you think has the most important job in a city? Why?

6. Who is the mayor of your city?

Write about It!

Describe what you would do to make your community better if you were elected mayor.

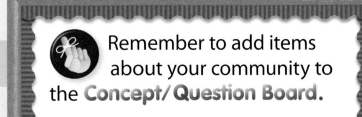

Remember to add items about your community to the **Concept/Question Board**.

LAWS

Laws are rules that everyone must follow. Countries, states, cities, and towns around the world have laws.

THE FIRST LAWS

When our country was new, there were no laws. A group of men met to find ways to make our country better. They helped write the Constitution.

LAWS KEEP US SAFE

Speed limits on roads are laws. Drivers must follow speed limits. A police officer can give a speeding driver a ticket. Tickets cost money.

LAWS KEEP US CLEAN

Other laws keep areas clean. In many places around the world, it is against the law to litter.

Good citizens follow laws. Laws are made to keep people safe and happy.

Think Link

1. How is the second heading helpful?

2. What is one law mentioned in the selection?

3. Why do countries make laws?

RESERVED PARKING

DISABLED PARKING REQUIRED

ONE WAY

STOP

NOT ER

Try It!

As you work on your investigation, think about how you could use headings to organize your information.

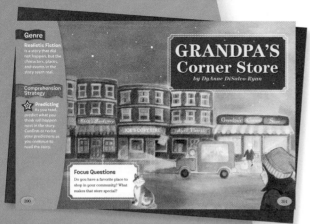

Read the article to find the meanings of these words, which are also in "Grandpa's Corner Store":

✦ arrangement
✦ tingle
✦ huddled
✦ sharp
✦ construction
✦ aisles

Vocabulary Strategy

Context Clues in the text help you find the meanings of words. Use context clues to find the meanings of *arrangement* and *huddled.*

388

Vocabulary

Warm-Up

Josh takes his dog for a walk almost every day. It is an arrangement he made with his mother. "You are in charge of Bosco," his mother reminds him.

Josh remembers the day he got Bosco. For a minute he feels that same tingle of excitement that he felt three years ago. He had wanted a dog for a very long time.

He went to the dog pound and saw Bosco huddled in the corner of a cage. Two other puppies were with him. Bosco had a droopy face and a wagging tail.

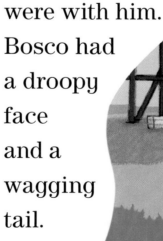

Josh feels a **sharp** yank on his pants. It is Bosco. "Okay, boy," Josh says. "Let's go for a walk." Just outside the door, Josh sees a hummingbird. Bosco's tail almost wags off. "Your tail flutters like that bird's wings," Josh laughs.

They make their way down the street and past the **construction**. Josh and Bosco head toward the pet store. It is the only store in town that lets dogs come inside. The store has more **aisles** than Josh can count.

It has more treats than Bosco can eat. "What a great store," says Josh. Bosco's tail wags faster than ever.

GAME

Sentence Building

Work with a partner to create sentences using the vocabulary words. Choose a word, and challenge your partner to make up a sentence using the word. Then switch roles. Continue until all the vocabulary words have been used.

Concept Vocabulary

The concept word for this lesson is **owner.** An *owner* is "someone who owns a business, such as a store or restaurant." What is your favorite store in your community? Have you ever talked to the owner of the store?

389

Focus Questions

Do you have a favorite place to shop in your community? What makes that store special?

GRANDPA'S
Corner Store

by DyAnne DiSalvo-Ryan

Grandpa's Corner Store

April Florist

NEWS

Mr. Butler sold his hardware store when a bigger one opened nearby. Then the building was torn down to make way for a new supermarket.

"Good luck," I say to Mr. Butler as he bumps his suitcase into his car.

"We'll miss you," my grandpa tells him. "*And* we'll miss your hardware store."

I hold on to Grandpa's hand, and we wave until Mr. Butler's car turns the corner.

Old stores are out. New stores are in. But my grandpa's store stays the same. A busy corner grocery with black and white tiles all worn straight down the middle aisle. Milk, juice, butter, eggs—the store has everything you need close by.

Grandpa lives in a room in the back. There's a bed for sleeping, a kitchen for cooking, and a cat named Shirley for company.

Saturday mornings I'm at the grocery to give Grandpa a hand. I stack the cans and sweep the aisles. Kids toss their bikes and skateboards outside and pile inside for candy. Firefighters from across the street line up at the deli counter. Mrs. Kalfo takes their orders and bags them up to go.

"I know, I know," Mrs. Kalfo says. "Cheese and pickle sandwiches. Hers on rye. His on wheat. Extra mayo on yours, right, chief?"

Chief Conley smiles at Grandpa. "She always gets it right."

The store is busy on Saturdays, so my mother comes in to help. Neighbors stop by to pick up what they need—a quart of milk, a box of cereal. Mr. Tutti comes in for yesterday's paper. He likes to take his time when he reads, so Grandpa saves it for him.

"So what do you think? With the new supermarket opening up, are you going to sell your store?" Mr. Tutti says flat out to my grandpa.

"Sell the grocery?" I look at Grandpa. "I don't think so," I tell Mr. Tutti. "My grandpa would never do that."

On Monday morning my teacher, Miss McCartney, tapes our neighborhood map on the board. We paste the library closest to the school, Korina's house farthest from Ira's.

"The new supermarket will have everything," Steven says without even raising his hand.

"My grandpa's store has everything already," I say a little bit louder than Miss McCartney would like.

But whatever I say that Grandpa's store has, Steven says the supermarket will have it too. Cheaper and bigger and better.

399

After school I stop for a minute to watch the construction work. My ears begin to tingle from the noise. Then all of a sudden I get this feeling that maybe Steven is right. The supermarket *is* going to be big. It was already much bigger than me.

"Lucy's here," Grandpa yells, waiting to give me my three o'clock hug. Mrs. Kalfo takes charge of the register. The table in the kitchen is set for homework, and Grandpa keeps me company. My mother says it's a nice arrangement to have while she's at work. I think so too.

"I'm making your corner grocery store to put on the neighborhood map at school," I say. Grandpa watches me color it in. "Steven is making the supermarket. He says your store is all washed up and you'll be moving to Florida, just like Mr. Butler."

Grandpa sighs and picks up a crayon. "Maybe Florida is nice," he says. "It's not so cold in the winter."

I laugh and give Grandpa a kiss. "Florida's too far away. You can't run your store from there."

When the telephone rings, it's Mr. Lee calling in an order.

"He's under the weather," my grandpa says.

I help pack the delivery bag. Bread, soup, coffee, noodles. Grandpa puts his coat on to go. Some deliveries are special, so he likes to do them himself.

I've finished coloring Grandpa's store
when my mother comes to get me. I toss
my crayons under the counter just before
I leave. That's when I see a red **FOR SALE**
sign hidden beneath some bags.

I can't even talk on the way home, but when we get inside, the words spill out.

"Is Grandpa selling his store?" I ask.

My mother sits us both in a chair. "Grandpa doesn't *want* to sell. He's afraid the new supermarket will put him out of business."

"Will Grandpa live with us if he sells?"

My mother looks around. "I'd like that more than anything," she says. "But we don't have the room."

I am just about to say he can have my room when I hear a knock at the door. Mrs. Kalfo stands in the hallway.

"Everybody's talking," Mrs. Kalfo says. She flutters her hands like a bird in a nest. "Everybody's worried the store will close."

"We're worried too," my mother says. "Come in. Sit down."

Mrs. Kalfo straightens her hat. "I guess, if it does, I'll try to get a job at the new supermarket. Things won't be the same for me anymore."

I throw my arms around my mother. "We have to do something," I say.

The next day, on the way to Grandpa's store, I try not to notice that the supermarket's going up fast. Construction workers call out to one another, waving steel beams into place. The sky is gray and thick with clouds. It almost feels like snow.

"Cold out there?" Mrs. Kalfo asks me, wrapping up a sandwich. Mrs. Duffy from down the block is huddled up talking to Grandpa.

"Pay when you can," I hear Grandpa whisper. Cheese, milk, diapers, bread.

Mrs. Duffy pats Grandpa's hand. "What would I do without you?" she says.

I bring my homework into the back and wait at the kitchen table.

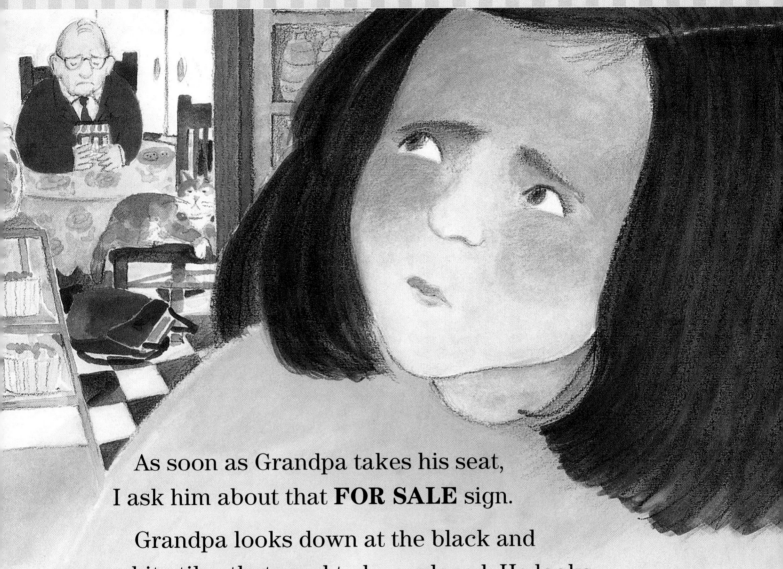

As soon as Grandpa takes his seat,
I ask him about that **FOR SALE** sign.

Grandpa looks down at the black and
white tiles that need to be replaced. He looks
up at a crack in the ceiling that needs to be
repaired. "The new supermarket will have
everything from soup to nuts," he tells me.

"But it won't have *you*." I hug my grandpa,
trying not to cry. I give him the grocery store
I colored in for school. "If you're really going
to sell your store, then you can keep this," I
say. "The map won't need it now."

The Saturday the roof goes up on the
supermarket, the **FOR SALE** sign goes up in
Grandpa's window. In school on Monday, I
won't even look at Steven. He keeps waving
around a flyer he ripped from a pole on the
avenue—

SUPERMARKET OPENS NEXT WEEK.

"I hope your grandpa likes Florida," he says, teasing. I grab the flyer out of his hand and throw it into the wastebasket.

We take turns pasting up more buildings. Somebody puts a tag with the words *mud pile* where the supermarket is being built, but Miss McCartney takes it down. I think that somebody is me.

"A community is a group of people who live and work together," Miss McCartney says, pointing to our map.

I think about what our community would be like without my grandpa's store.

And then I look at Steven and smile. Miss McCartney has given me an idea.

Fancy Restaurant   wei   Jewelry Store   MUD PILE

"Be there Saturday morning," I tell all the kids on my way home after school.

"Nine o'clock sharp," the firefighters say.

"I'll help spread the word," says Mr. Tutti.

"Not a problem."
Mr. Lee sneezes.

Mrs. Kalfo pats my arm. "You can count on me," she says.

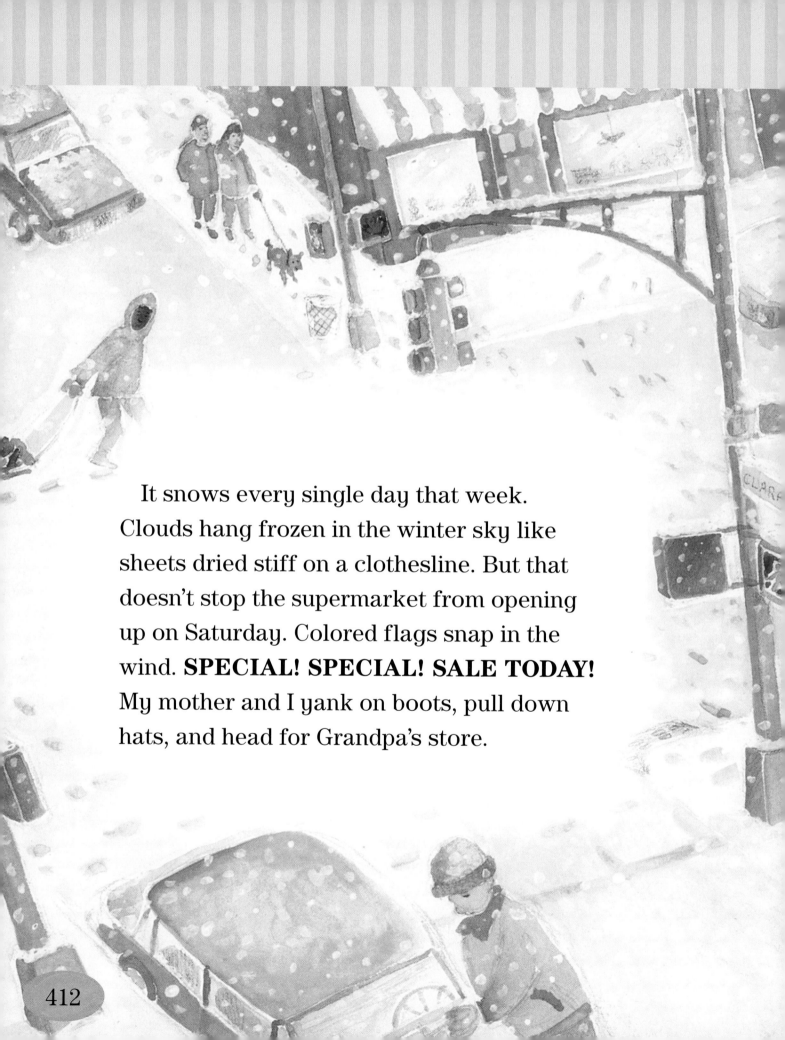

It snows every single day that week. Clouds hang frozen in the winter sky like sheets dried stiff on a clothesline. But that doesn't stop the supermarket from opening up on Saturday. Colored flags snap in the wind. **SPECIAL! SPECIAL! SALE TODAY!** My mother and I yank on boots, pull down hats, and head for Grandpa's store.

"I hope this works,"
I tell my mother as we
brave our way around
the corner.

Neighbors are bunched in front of the
grocery all packed up like snowballs.
"Here comes Lucy!" Chief Conley waves.

Mr. Lee is pouring out coffee. Mrs. Duffy
has her five kids bundled up onto a sled.

Mrs. Kalfo is laughing. "Your grandpa can't see us. His windows are all iced up."

There's the carpenter's truck, the kids from school—even Miss McCartney's here.

I take a deep breath and push the door open.

"Where is everybody?" I ask Grandpa, trying to keep the secret.

"Probably at the supermarket," he says. "Who needs this place now?"

"You'd be surprised," I tell my grandpa.

That's when the old front door claps open, cheering for everyone as they come in. Neighbors are carrying paint cans, black and white tiles, nails and hammers, and plaster mix. Some of the people I don't even know.

"What's all this?" my grandpa asks.

"It's Lucy's idea," Mrs. Kalfo says. "We're all here to spruce up this place."

"Did you really think we'd let you get away so fast?" Chief Conley asks my grandpa.

"Who's going to make my deliveries special?" Mr. Lee wants to know.

"And what about our cheese and pickle sandwiches?" the firefighters remind Grandpa.

"And you know me," Mr. Tutti says. "I need yesterday's news today."

"Do you still want this?" I ask Grandpa, taking down the **FOR SALE** sign.

Grandpa looks around his store. People keep coming in left and right, banging their feet, rubbing their hands, and getting to work. Grandpa walks into the kitchen and comes out holding my colored-in grocery store.

"Thank you, Lucy," he whispers, handing it back to me. "I think your map will need this now." Then Grandpa hugs me, broom and all.

Well, the grand opening of the new supermarket was a huge success. Steven was right. The supermarket is big. But it isn't bigger than a whole neighborhood.

In school Steven pastes a big rectangle on our map and marks it "supermarket."

I raise my hand. "Bigger but not better," I tell Miss McCartney. Then I paste my grandpa's grocery store right around the corner from my house. Milk, juice, butter, eggs—it has everything you need close by. And best of all, it has Grandpa.

Meet the Author and Illustrator

DyAnne DiSalvo-Ryan

DiSalvo-Ryan wanted to illustrate books ever since she was eight years old; she was reading a book and decided she could do a better job. She has illustrated many books that other people have written and has also written and illustrated some of her own books. DiSalvo-Ryan gets inspiration for her stories and drawings from her friends, family, and people she passes on the street. Listening to different kinds of music helps her with her work too.

FANCY Restaurant

MUD PILE

wei

Theme Connections

Within the Selection

1. Why does Lucy's grandpa think he should sell his store?

2. What makes Lucy's grandpa decide to keep the store?

Across Selections

3. How are Pablo from "Jalapeño Bagels" and Lucy alike?

Beyond the Selection

4. How can large supermarkets and small corner stores stay in business in the same community?

Jewelry Store

Write about It!

Describe a grocery store in your community. Is it a big supermarket or a small corner store?

Remember to look for pictures of grocery stores to add to the **Concept/ Question Board.**

How I Get to School

Some kids ride the bus to school, but not me. I walk. Mom and I have an arrangement every year. We talk about how I am going to get to school. I even draw a map that shows the best way to go. I start with my house on Vine Street. I put a big "X" on my house to show where I will start or end each day.

After I draw my house on Vine Street, I draw an arrow that shows I will go to Oak Street and turn left. There is a big pond on Oak Street. I draw the pond on my map.

Next I turn right on Maple Street. There is a fire station on the corner. I draw the fire station on my map. I even draw fire engines. This makes my map more interesting.

My school is at 297 Maple Street. I mark my school with a big "X," just like my house. Now my house and school are important places on the map.

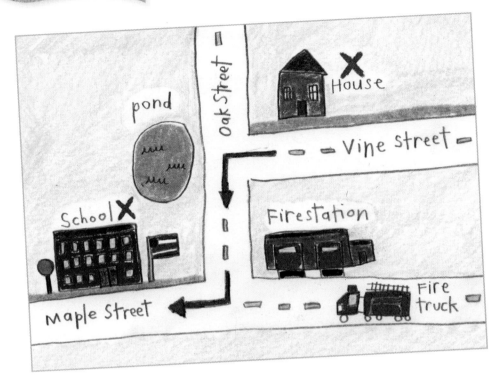

1. What word in the first sentence lets you know this story is a narrative?

2. How can a map help a person get somewhere?

3. Why might a person mark a spot on the map with an "X"?

Try It!

As you work on your investigation, think about how you could use a map to show your facts.

SUPERMARKET

by Lois Lenski

illustrated by Joe Cepeda

The supermarket is a place
    With food piled very high,
On shelves and counters all around,
    Where people come to buy.

They push a cart and help themselves
    To cookies, meat and pie;
Turnips, pickles, canned goods, bread—
    They fill the cart up high.

Then when they leave, go through a gate,
    A checker checks them through;
They pay their bill, pick up the bags—
    That's all they have to do.

The supermarket is a store
    With every food complete,
Where people pick out what they want,
    And take it home to eat.

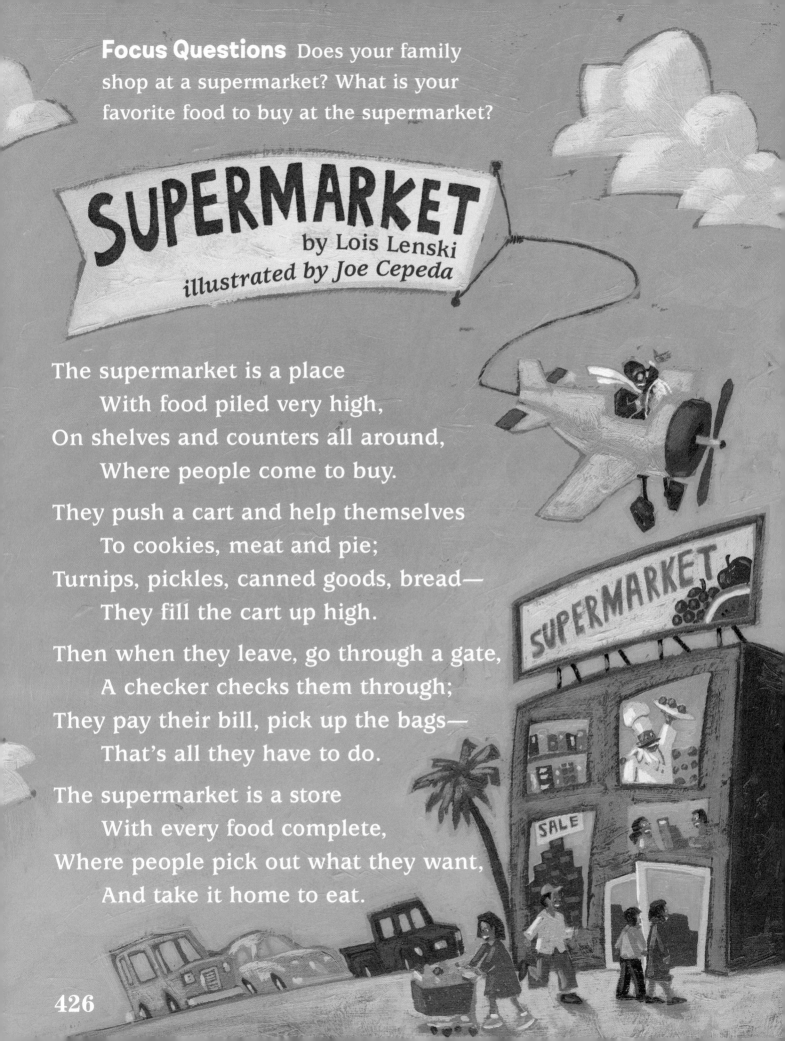

426

Focus Questions

What types of books do
you look for at the library?
What is your favorite book?

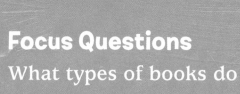

THE LIBRARY

by Barbara A. Huff
illustrated by Joe Cepeda

It looks like any building
When you pass it on the street,
Made of stone and glass
    and marble,
Made of iron and concrete.

But once inside you can ride
A camel or a train,
Visit Rome, Siam, or Nome,
Feel a hurricane,
Meet a king, learn to sing,
How to bake a pie,
Go to sea, plant a tree
Find how airplanes fly,
Train a horse, and of course
Have all the dogs you'd like,
See the moon, a sandy dune,
Or catch a whopping pike.
Everything that books can bring
You'll find inside those walls.
A world is there for you to share
When adventure calls.

You cannot tell its magic
By the way the building looks,
But there's wonderment within it,
The wonderment of books.

427

Test Prep

Be sure to look at all the answers to a question. Think about what the question is asking. Compare the answers to one another. Choose the one you think is best.

Comparing Answer Choices

It is important to look carefully at every answer when you take a test. Choose the answer that is best.

EXAMPLE

Read this sentence and the answer choices. Compare all the answer choices. Decide which answer fits best in the blank.

1. Nancy put her _____ in her backpack. She was on her way to school.
   ○ toys
   ○ books
   ○ shoes

Compare the answer choices, and think about the sentence. If Nancy is getting ready for school, she will probably put *books* in her backpack. *Books* is a better choice than the others, and it makes sense with the sentence.

Around Town

"Do you want to go for a walk?" asks George. "We will not go far."

"I guess," says Tory. "There is not much to do here."

Tory is George's cousin. She is from a big city. George lives in a small town. This is Tory's first visit.

They walk for two blocks. George takes Tory to a bakery, and they go inside. It smells wonderful. George buys a loaf of bread for dinner. Then they share a bagel that the bakery owner gave them.

"That was fun," says Tory. "I do not think I have ever tasted a bagel like that." She looks at a building across the street. "What building is that? It is pretty."

GO ON

George leads her across the street. "That is our town hall," he says. "It is almost two hundred years old." George feels a little proud.

Tory walks up the steps. She looks at the pretty windows. They are made of pieces of colored glass.

"Let's walk home through the park," says George. "I have a surprise."

They turn the corner. The park is between the town hall and George's house. In the middle of the park are a fountain and a pond. They walk over to it.

"Wow," says Tory. "This is beautiful. Look at all the fish. I had no idea a little town could be so cool."

1. This story is probably a _____.

    ○ fairy tale

    ○ fable

    ○ poem

    ○ true story

2. Who is Tory?

    ○ A neighbor

    ○ George's cousin

    ○ A family friend

    ○ George's sister

3. The windows in the town hall are _____.

    ○ made of colored glass

    ○ open just a little

    ○ too high to see through

    ○ covered with cloth

4. What does George buy?

    ○ Bagels

    ○ Eggs

    ○ Bread

    ○ Milk

5. Where do the children go last?

    ○ To the bakery

    ○ To the park

    ○ To the town hall

    ○ To the big city

Test Tips

- Listen to the directions carefully.

- Compare all the answer choices before choosing the one that best answers the question.

- Identify the important words in the questions.

STOP

Pronunciation Key

a as in **a**t
ā as in l**a**te
â as in c**a**re
ä as in f**a**ther
e as in s**e**t
ē as in m**e**
i as in **i**t
ī as in k**i**te
o as in **o**x
ō as in r**o**se

ô as in b**o**ught and r**a**w
oi as in c**oi**n
o͞o as in b**oo**k
o͞o as in t**oo**
or as in f**or**m
ou as in **ou**t
u as in **u**p
ū as in **u**se
ûr as in t**ur**n, g**er**m, l**ear**n, f**ir**m, w**or**k

ə as in **a**bout, chick**e**n, p**e**ncil, cann**o**n, circ**u**s
ch as in **ch**air
hw as in **wh**ich
ng as in ri**ng**
sh as in **sh**op
th as in **th**in
t͟h as in **th**ere
zh as in trea**s**ure

The mark (ˊ) is placed after a syllable with a heavy accent, as in **chicken** (chikˊ ən).

The mark (ˏ) after a syllable shows a lighter accent, as in **disappear** (disˊ ə pērˊ).

Glossary

A

absorbs (ab sôrbs´) *v.* Soaks up.

admiring (ad mīr´ ing) *v.* Being happy with.

aisles (īlz) *n.* Plural of **aisle:** the space between two rows or sections of something.

amazement (ə mā´ zmənt) *n.* A strong feeling of wonder or surprise.

amazing (ə mā´ zing) *adj.* Surprising.

ancestors (an´ ses tərz) *n.* Plural of **ancestor:** a person from whom one is descended.

anchor (ang´ kər) *v.* To hold steadily and in place.

antennae (an ten´ ə) *n.* Plural of **antenna:** an insect feeler.

anthill (ant´ hil) *n.* A mound of soil, sand, or dirt formed by ants.

anthill

arrangement (ə rānj´ mənt) *n.* A plan.

attract (ə trakt´) *v.* To draw attention.

automatically (ô´ tə mat´ ic ə´ lē) *adv.* Working by itself.

B

bakery (bāk´ ər ē) *n.* A building where items of food, especially bread and cakes, are baked and sold.

Pronunciation Key: at; lāte; câre; fäther; set; mē; it; kīte; ox; rōse; ô in bought; coin; book; too; form; out; up; ūse; tûrn; ə sound in about, chicken, pencil, cannon, circus; chair; hw in which; ring; shop; thin; there; zh in treasure

basic (bā´ sik) *adj*. Very important.

batch (bach) *n*. The amount of something baked at one time.

boils (boilz) *v*. Heats so that bubbles form and steam is given off.

boils

borrow (bôr´ ō) *v*. To receive something with the understanding that it must be given back.

broadleaf (brôd´ lēf) *n*. A kind of tree that has flat, wide leaves.

budget (buj´ it) *n*. A summary of income and spending.

butterflies (bu´ tûr flīz´) *n*. Plural of **butterfly**: a fluttering feeling in the stomach caused by nervousness.

byway (bī´ wā) *n*. A small side road.

C

care (kâr) *v*. To look after.

cashier (ka shir´) *n*. A person in charge of paying out or receiving money.

chain (chān) *n*. A row of connected or related circles.

charge (chärj) *v*. To be responsible for.

cheeps (chēps) *n*. Plural of **cheep**: a sound made by a young bird.

clicking (klik´ ing) *v.* Making a short, sharp sound.

cocoon (kə koon´) *n.* A case that protects an insect while it changes to an adult.

cocoon

colonies (kol´ ə nēs) *n.* Plural of **colony:** a group of plants or animals.

comb (kōm) *v.* To search an area thoroughly.

completely (kəm plēt´ lē) *adv.* Entirely.

construction (kən struk´ shən) *n.* The act of building something.

council (koun´ səl) *n.* A group of people who make decisions for a larger group.

creep (krēp) *v.* To move slowly and quietly.

crinkle (kring´ kəl) *v.* To scrunch up.

crook (krook) *n.* A bent or curved part of something.

culture (kul´ chər) *n.* The customs and beliefs of a group of people.

curtain (kûr´ tin) *n.* A piece of cloth hung across a window.

customers (kus´ tə mərz) *n.* Plural of **customer:** a person who buys goods or services.

cycle (sī´ kəl) *n.* A repeated sequence of events.

dashing (dash´ ing) *v.* Running suddenly.

dough

dawn (dôn) *n.* The time each morning at which daylight first begins.

deposits (di poz´ itz) *n.* Plural of **deposit:** money added to a bank account.

deserted (di zûrt´ ed) *v.* Past tense of **desert:** to leave something behind.

destroyed (di stroid´) *v.* Past tense of **destroy:** to get rid of.

different (dif´ ər ənt) *adj.* Not the same as something or somebody else.

dough (dō) *n.* A mixture of flour, liquid, and other things that is usually baked.

dull (dul) *adj.* Not bright or clear.

dusk (dusk) *n.* The time of day just before the sun goes down.

dusty (dust´ ē) *adj.* Covered with dirt.

eager (ē´ gər) *adj.* Showing excitement and interest.

elect (i lekt´) *v.* To choose by voting.

elves (elvz) *n.* Plural of **elf:** a type of fairy.

employees (em ploi´ ēz) *n.* Plural of **employee:** a person who works for a person or business for pay.

enemies (en´ ə mēs) *n.* Plural of **enemy:** a person or thing that wants to hurt another.

engines (en´ jinz) *n.* Plural of **engine:** a machine that uses energy to run other machines.

engine

enormous (i nôr´ məs) *adj.* Very big.

escalator (es´ kə lā´ tər) *n.* Moving stairs.

events (i ventz´) *n.* Plural of **event:** something that takes place.

evergreen (ev´ ər grēn´) *n.* A kind of tree that does not lose its leaves.

evergreen

everlasting (ev´ ər las´ ting) *adj.* Lasting forever.

examined (ig zam´ ind) *v.* Past tense of **examine:** to look at closely and carefully.

exclaimed (iks klāmd´) *v.* Past tense of **exclaim:** to speak out suddenly.

extremely (ek strēm´ lē) *adv.* Very.

fastened (fas´ ənd) *v.* Past tense of **fasten:** to button.

fee (fē) *n.* Money paid for a service.

feelings (fē´ lingz) *n.* Plural of **feeling:** an emotion, such as joy, fear, sadness.

finest (fī´ nest) *adj.* Nicest.

flash (flash) *n.* An instant.

flashed (flashd) *v.* Past tense of **flash:** to move suddenly or quickly.

flutters (flut´ ərz) *v.* Waves or flaps with quick movements.

flyer (flī´ ər) *n.* A small, paper advertisement.

fossil (fôs´ əl) *n.* Preserved remains.

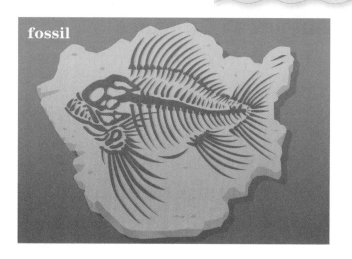
fossil

furious (fyûr´ ē əs) *adj.* Very angry.

fussy (fus´ ē) *adj.* Hard to please.

gasped (gaspt) *v.* Past tense of **gasp:** to speak breathlessly.

glows (glōz) *v.* Shines.

gnaw (nô) *v.* To chew.

grow (grō) *v.* To get bigger.

hardware (härd´ wâr) *n.* Metal tools for making and fixing things.

harvest (här´ vist) *v.* To gather crops when they are ripe.

help (help) *v.* To do something useful, wanted, or needed.

huddled (hud´ dəld) *v.* Past tense of **huddle:** to crowd together.

ideas (ī dē´ əs) *n.* Plural of **idea:** a picture or thought formed in the mind.

important (im pôr´ tənt) *adj.* Having great value or meaning.

ingredients (in grē´ dē əntz) *n.* Plural of **ingredient:** a part that goes into a mixture.

ingredients

inner (in´ ər) *adj.* Inside.

insects (in´ sektz) *n.* Plural of **insect:** a six-legged bug.

insist (in sist´) *v.* To demand.

interest (in´ tər əst) *n.* The cost of borrowing money or a payment made for the use of money.

international (in´ tər nash´ ə nəl) *adj.* Having to do with two or more nations.

invade (in vād´) *v.* To enter without an invitation.

J

jalapeño (hoˊlə pāˊnyō) *n.* A small, hot pepper.

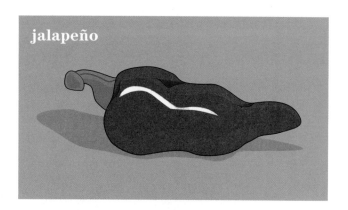

jalapeño

K

kind (kīnd) *adj.* Gentle, giving, and friendly.

knead (nēd) *v.* To mix and press together a soft substance, such as dough, with the hands.

L

larva (larˊvə) *n.* The wingless form of many insects before they become adults.

learn (lûrn) *v.* To come to know something.

leather (let/hˊər) *n.* Material made from the skin of an animal.

limbs (limz) *n.* Plural of **limb:** a branch of a tree.

litter (litˊər) *n.* Scattered paper and other materials; trash.

loan (lōn) *n.* Money given to somebody on the condition that it will be paid back later.

lobby (lob´ ē) *n.* A hall or room near the entrance to a building.

lobby

lox (lokz) *n.* Smoked salmon.

mad (mad) *adj.* Wild and excited.

manager (man´ i jər) *n.* A person who is responsible for directing and controlling the work of a business.

mayor (mā´ ər) *n.* The person who is the head of a city or town government.

midnight (mid´ nīt´) *n.* Twelve o'clock at night.

minerals (min´ ər əlz) *n.* Plural of **mineral:** something found underground and used as food for plants growing in soil.

minutes (min´ itz) *n.* Written notes that tell what took place at a meeting.

molting (mōlt´ ing) *v.* Losing feathers or skin.

needless (nēd´ lis) *adj.* Not necessary.

nurture (nûr´ chər) *v.* To give tender care to somebody or something to help it grow.

nymphs (nimfz) *n.* Plural of **nymph:** a young insect.

outer (ou´ tər) *adj.* Outside.

outstretched (out strecht´) *adj.* Reaching out.

441

overalls (ō´ vər ôlz´) *n.* Pants with a bib front and straps at the shoulders.

oxygen (ok´ si jən) *n.* A gas that has no color or smell.

P

palace (pal´ is) *n.* A large, fancy house.

palpi (pal´ pē) *n.* Small feelers on a grasshopper's mouth that hold and taste food.

paste (pāst) *n.* A thick, soft mixture of wet and dry ingredients.

pavement (pāv´ mənt) *n.* The hard surface of a road, street, or sidewalk.

peace (pēs) *n.* Freedom from fighting or conflict.

peacefully (pēs´ fəl lē) *adv.* Calmly.

pebbles (peb´ əlz) *n.* Plural of **pebble:** a small rounded stone.

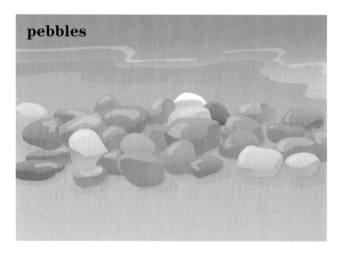

pebbles

peeked (pēkt) *v.* Past tense of **peek:** to take a quick look at something.

perch (pûrch) *n.* A place for a bird to land or rest.

perched (pûrcht) *v.* Past tense of **perch:** to stand, sit, or rest on a raised place.

photosynthesis (fō´ tə sin´ thə sis) *n.* The process by which green plants use carbon dioxide, water, and sunlight to make their own food.

pigeons (pij´ ənz) *n.* Plural of **pigeon:** a bird with a plump body, a small head, and thick, soft feathers

pile (pīl) *n.* A number of things lying one on top of the other.

plump (plump) *adj.* Round and full.

poison (poi´ zən) *n.* A substance that causes death or injury.

practice (prak´ tis) *v.* To do something over and over to gain skill.

precious (presh´ əs) *adj.* Loved and cherished.

print (print) *n.* A mark made by pressing.

public (pub´ lik) *adj.* For all the people.

pumpernickel (pump´ ər nik´ əl) *n.* A dark, dense, slightly sour bread.

puny (pū´ nē) *adj.* Small and weak.

pupa (pū´ pə) *n.* An insect at the stage before it is an adult.

raged (rājd) *v.* Past tense of **rage:** to act violently.

receipt (ri sēt´) *n.* A written statement showing that something has been received.

recipe (res´ ə pē´) *n.* A list of ingredients and instructions for making something to eat or drink.

recognize (rek´ əg nīz´) *v.* To know and remember from before.

register (rəj´ ə stər) *n.* A machine that records sales, calculates totals, and has a drawer for money.

register

release (ri lēs´) *v.* To give off.

rent (rent) *n.* A regular payment for the right to use equipment or property that belongs to someone else.

repay (ri pā´) *v.* To pay or give back.

routes (routz) *n.* Plural of **route:** a road or other course used for traveling.

S

sap (sap) *n.* A watery liquid containing minerals and nutrients that flow through trees and other plants.

scampered (scam´ pərd) *v.* Past tense of **scamper:** to run quickly.

sensing (sens´ ing) *v.* Feeling.

services (ser´ vis əz) *n.* Plural of **service:** work done by somebody for somebody else.

share (shâr) *v.* To divide into portions and give to others as well as to oneself.

sharp (sharp) *adj.* Exact.

shoemaker (shoo´ mā´ kər) *n.* Someone who makes shoes.

sighed (sīd) *v.* Past tense of **sigh**: to let out a deep breath in relief or sadness.

silky (sil´kē) *adj.* Shiny and soft.

skipped (skipt) *v.* Past tense of **skip**: to move along by hopping from one foot to the other.

skyscraper (skī´skrā´pər) *n.* A very tall building.

skyscraper

snoozing (snūz´ing) *v.* Taking a quick nap.

snug (snug) *adj.* Warm and comfortable.

sorting (sôrt´ing) *v.* Putting into groups according to kind or type.

spark (spärk) *v.* To give off flashes of light.

sprouts (sprouts) *v.* Begins to grow.

spruce up (sprūs up) *v.* To make clean and neat.

squeaked (skwēkd) *v.* Past tense of **squeak**: to make a short high sound or cry.

squirt (skwûrt) *v.* To push out in a thin stream.

stalking (stôk´ing) *v.* Following someone or something quietly and carefully in order to catch it.

stamp (stamp) *v.* To mark with a tool that makes or prints a design, numbers, or letters.

steep (stēp) *adj.* Having a sharp slope.

stems (stemz) *n.* Plural of **stem**: the main part of a plant.

still (stil) *adj.* Quiet.

Pronunciation Key: at; l**ā**te; c**â**re; f**ä**ther; s**e**t; m**ē**; **i**t; k**ī**te; **o**x; r**ō**se; **ô** in b**ou**ght; c**oi**n; b**oo**k; t**oo**; f**or**m; **ou**t; **u**p; **ū**se; t**û**rn; **ə** sound in **a**bout, chick**e**n, penc**i**l, cann**o**n, circ**u**s; **ch**air; **hw** in **wh**ich; ri**ng**; **sh**op; **th**in; **th**ere; **zh** in trea**s**ure

stitched (stichd) *v.* Past tense of **stitch:** to sew.

store (stôr) *v.* To put away for future use.

stripe (strīp) *n.* A long, narrow band that differs in color, composition, or texture from the surrounding surface.

stripe

supermarket (soo´ pər mär´ kət) *n.* A large store that sells food and household goods.

surface (sûr´ fis) *n.* The top part of something.

taxes (taks´ əz) *n.* Plural of **tax:** money that people or businesses must pay to support the government.

teach (tēch) *v.* To give knowledge to somebody by instruction or example.

tenants (ten´ ənts) *n.* Plural of **tenant:** one who lives in or on another person's property.

tiddly (ti´ dlē) *adj.* Very small.

tiles (tīlz) *n.* Plural of **tile:** a thin, flat piece of hard material used for covering roofs, floors, or walls.

tingle (ting´ gəl) *v.* To have a slight stinging feeling.

towers (tou´ ərz) v. To be very high or tall.

trace (trās) v. To follow the path of something.

transaction (tran zak´ shən) n. An exchange of money, goods, or services.

transportation (trans´ pər tā´ shən) n. The act of carrying or moving something from one place to another.

trunks (trungks) n. Plural of **trunk:** the main part of a tree where the branches grow out.

trunk

tunnels (tun´ əlz) n. Plural of **tunnel:** an underground passageway.

underneath (un´ dər nēth´) adv. Below.

usual (ū´ zhoo əl) adj. Regular.

vacant (vā´ kənt) adj. Empty.

vacated (vā´ cā təd) v. Past tense of **vacate:** to leave empty.

vault (volt) n. A room or compartment used to store money or other things of value.

wandered (won´ dərd) v. Past tense of **wander:** to move from place to place.

withdrawals (with drôlz´) n. Plural of **withdrawal:** money taken out of a bank account.

447

Pronunciation Key: at; lāte; câre; fäther; set; mē; it; kīte; ox; rōse; ô in bought; coin; bŏŏk; tōō; form; out; up; ūse; tûrn; ə sound in about, chicken, pencil, cannon, circus; chair; hw in which; ring; shop; thin; there; zh in treasure

witness (wit´ nis) *v.* To see or hear something.

yanked (yangkt) *v.* Past tense of **yank:** to pull.